D0712086

Hello

BROKEN STAR

The Story of the League of Nations
(1919-1939)

COMMUNITY LIBRARY CENTER
SAN LEANDRO, CALIFORNIA

BROKEN STAR

The Story of the League of Nations
(1919-1939)

JAMES AVERY JOYCE

"All efforts to make the nations live and work together are still in their infancy. We cannot even say that the definite forms they will take are clearly before us, but the road at least by which we must progress is visible."

Gustav Stresemann (1928)

Christopher Davies
Swansea

341.22

[c 1978]

Copyright © James Avery Joyce 1978
Published in 1978 by
Christopher Davies (Publishers) Ltd
52 Mansel Street
Swansea SA1 5EL

*All rights reserved. No part of this publication may
be reproduced, stored in a retrieval system, or
transmitted, in any form or by any means,
electronic, mechanical, photocopying, recording
or otherwise, without the prior permission of
Christopher Davies (Publishers) Ltd*

*Printed in Wales by
Salesbury Press Ltd
Llandybïe, Dyfed*

ISBN 0 7154 0419 9

For

PHILIP NOEL-BAKER

Nobel Peace Prize Winner, who brought to the League what the statesmen denied it, faith and loyalty

By the same author:

WORLD OF PROMISE
REVOLUTION ON EAST RIVER
END OF AN ILLUSION
CHALLENGE OF THE DECADE OF DEVELOPMENT
RED CROSS INTERNATIONAL
NOW IS THE TIME
JUSTICE AT WORK
CAPITAL PUNISHMENT: A WORLD VIEW
YOUTH FACES THE NEW WORLD
THE NEW POLITICS OF HUMAN RIGHTS
WORLD POPULATION: BASIC DOCUMENTS
HUMAN RIGHTS: INTERNATIONAL DOCUMENTS
JOBS *versus* PEOPLE (I.L.O.)
LABOUR FACES THE NEW AGE (I.L.O.)
EDUCATION AND TRAINING (UNITED NATIONS)
STUDIES IN U.N. CHARTER REVISION (ED.)
WORLD ORGANIZATION — FEDERAL OR FUNCTIONAL
    (SYMPOSIUM)

Acknowledgements

It is impossible in a survey of real events covering some twenty years to record or even recall the personalities who have shaped this narrative. I never met President Woodrow Wilson, for he never came to Geneva to see his league at work; but I saw Mrs Wilson several times in her front seat in the Assembly gallery. I met and talked with Nansen, Herriot, Hymans and other leading statesmen who came regularly to Geneva, as well as members of the British group: Arthur Henderson, Hugh Dalton, Cecil Hurst and Gilbert Murray, while Lord Robert Cecil wrote the preface to my first book in 1931: *Youth Faces the New World*.

Among my teachers and mentors were Sir Alfred Zimmern, Professor William Rappard, Senor de Madriaga (then head of the League's Disarmament Section) and not least, Philip Noel-Baker, whose courses on Diplomatic History I attended at L.S.E. As regards journalists and writers, Vernon Bartlett, the League's most brilliant commentator and pioneer of BBC talks on world affairs, introduced me to my first writing assignments in Geneva, while quite half the authors, whose contemporary works I have cited, were part of my Geneva intellectual upbringing.

I have, in fact, relied on their contemporaneous reflexions on the League rather than on the few mainly critical commentaries that have appeared since the Second World War (and included in my booklist), since I wanted the League story to be my story, not someone else's. Into my office in England as an adult education lecturer on world affairs and later an official of the League of Nations Union, came a daily spate of reports, brochures, magazines and correspondence on the League.

Finally, my long-standing friend, Emery Kelen, has generously permitted me to reproduce some of his world-famous caricatures, and Mr Welander, the chief Geneva archivist, assisted me with photographs selected from the U.N. and the ILO libraries, whose kindness I gratefully acknowledge.   J.A.J.

Contents

Why Study the League?

For centuries, men have dreamed of an earth that Tennyson envisioned as—

> "The Federation of the World
> And the Parliament of Man."

Thinkers and statesmen, appalled by the horrors and futility of ever-recurring warfare, have from time to time thought up plans for the abolition of war and a world organised around the idea of the brotherhood of Man.

For example, the poet Dante in 1309 proposed in his book *The Kingdom* that all nations should live under one law and that this 'world law' would one day keep nations from going to war with each other. Two hundred years later the Dutch scholar Erasmus in his *Complaint of Peace* appealed to all earthly kings and rulers to set up a Council of Just Men to deal with disputes so that (as he put it) 'wars shall not breed wars'. At the end of the 16th century the Duc de Sully wrote the *Grand Design* suggesting that the 15 States of Europe set up a Council of Europe to deal with the problems arising between them like a national parliament would. Hugo Grotius, in 1625, set out in his *Laws of War and Peace* the first comprehensive system of international law. William Penn drew up a scheme in 1693 for a European Parliament, and Abbé de Saint-Pierre in 1716 devised a *Project for Permanent Peace* to unite the nations' rulers in a Senate, where voting would take the place of war-making. Jean-Jacques Rousseau and Immanuel Kant and many others dreamed up the kind of world order, in the light of their times, which would abolish war and bring the nations together as one family. And so on down to our own times. The 19th century was full of such ideas and schemes.

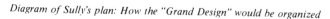

Diagram of Sully's plan: How the "Grand Design" would be organized

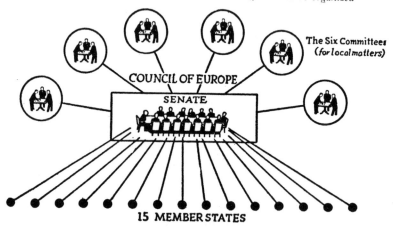

But, for the first time, following the First World War, which lasted from 1914 to 1918, a world legal constitution was actually drawn up *and agreed* at the Peace Conference in Paris. The Covenant of the League of Nations, as it was called, was included as part of the Treaty of Versailles, which was signed in June, 1919. This Covenant consisted of 26 articles (summarised on page x) and it came into effect on January 20, 1920, when the League began to function at its headquarters in Geneva.

61 nations eventually joined the League, but not the United States. The League continued as a major force in the world's life until the Second World War started in September, 1939. No-one can usefully follow modern history between the two World Wars without a clear knowledge of what the League of Nations was and did. Although it was never a world parliament, as we regard national parliaments, many people today recognise it as the true parent of the present United Nations, to which it passed on its chief functions in 1946, a year after the U.N. was formed.

Its twenty years were filled with intense activity. The League tackled a score of small conflicts which might have become world wars, if agreed international action had not stopped them in time. It brought together the leading statesmen of the time in annual sessions of the Assembly. This Assembly met at Geneva and consisted of three delegates appointed by each of the Member States. At the height of its influence, over 40 prime ministers and foreign ministers would regularly attend its sessions; while its committees were staffed by over a thousand experts and a trained secretariat who were nationals drawn from nearly 60 countries. It could not pass 'laws' in the ordinary sense of the word, but its resolutions marked the highest point that international co-operation could reach in the circumstances.

Alongside the annual Assemblies, a Council met at frequent intervals, especially when a conflict or crisis swept the news headlines of the world. Again, a dozen or more Foreign Ministers, or their deputies, composed the Council of the League. When it is recalled that, among a host of lesser problems, the Japanese invasion of China, the Italian invasion of Ethiopia, and the German invasion of Austria and Czechoslovakia (which led directly to the Second World War) came before this Council, it is evident that the League had become the mirror of a very discordant world.

Why could not the League handle and control these major crises? That is one of the questions to which we must give close attention in this book. For all this looks very similar to the problems of the present United Nations which has its General Assembly, Security Council, Committees, and Secretariat, on the same basic pattern as the League. In fact, we shall find many comparisons and likenesses with the U.N. and thereby realise how close the League experiment comes to explaining and elucidating many of the present-day activities under the United Nations Charter.

But the League also has to be seen against its background in history. One of the most interesting aspects of the League experiment was the way in which it drastically transformed the old 'balance of power' system, going back to the Congress of

Vienna, following the defeat of Napoleon in 1815. This new system was called 'collective security' and the Covenant attempted to set up the rules by which all its members came to the assistance of any member who was attacked by an aggressor. But, as the facts unfortunately showed, what went wrong with the League was that 'collective security' under the Covenant never worked.

While we must give full weight in this book to the epoch-making initiative and courage displayed by President Woodrow Wilson in founding the League, it is also necessary to assess the nature of the tragedy which dogged the steps of the League when the United States declined to join it.

Much of current world history was reflected in the League's deliberations during these two decades, but only those events that directly affected the activities of the League can be covered in the following chapters. For that reason our study will necessarily centre chiefly on European politics in general and British, French, and German diplomacy in particular.

*   *   *   *   *

It might be thought that there is nothing new today to be said about the League of Nations. There was a time — between the two World Wars — when a great deal was said and written about the Geneva organization. But, after a quarter of a century of the United Nations, what can be said about its predecessor (runs the argument) except that it was, at best, a glorious failure?

Not that the League is altogether ignored today. It often comes up as a kind of warning, or by way of contrast to or comparison with the U.N. Then, there have been so many books and articles written during the last decade or so explaining what went wrong with the world to produce Hitler's war. This revival of reminiscent 'war' books and about the years leading up to World War II, never fails to discredit the League. Why did it not stop Japan going into China, prevent Italy from invading Ethiopia, deter Germany from annexing Austria? And there was the fateful Munich crisis, the Russian-German pact, and so on. Where was the League in all this? And, since the United States stayed out, what was the *use* of the League anyway?

A new generation has since grown up which never knew the League. They — the young generation — think of it, if at all, as something that happened before they were born, and which has no more relevance today than the battle of Waterloo or the Indian Mutiny. In fact, it receives passing notice in newspaper editorials more for what it failed to do than for what it *did*.

Even then, its memory is buried under a heap of errors — errors of fact, as well as of historical judgment. Some teachers think nothing of telling modern history students that the League 'packed up' when the 'aggressors' got out of hand or when Japan or Italy or Germany resigned. That the League was not dissolved until 1946 — a year after the U.N. was founded — and that some sections of it continued functioning throughout World War II, did not seem to matter, so were ignored. But the fact is that the flying start that the U.N. made was largely due to the team of experienced and competent men and women who were carried over into the new Organization.

No-one seems to credit the fact either that, *before* the 'aggressors' began to break up the League, it was the world economic crisis, round about 1930 (which had its origin in the United States), that hit the League like a cyclone, and from which it could never recover. In fact, each of the major aggressors were motivated, in turn, by the economic *malaise* of the 1930's. This forgotten piece of economic history will receive particular analysis in the present book; it is a key to unlock the dark tragedies of the League's later years.

It is most significant that, unlike the League, its successor was structured to tackle the economic and social needs of mankind, so that, today, 85 per cent of the U.N. staff have their jobs in the economic and technological sphere. The U.N. diverges more and more away from the preoccupations of pre-War Geneva, and this aspect, too, will be strongly underlined as the narrative proceeds. The League stood at the transition between modern history and contemporary history, a transition that closed some doors forever, while it opened others into the twenty-first century.

Yet the League, in its time, carried out astonishingly well a long list of humanitarian tasks — slavery, refugees, health, education, child welfare. The story is an enheartening one and millions owed their very existence to it. Not least, the International Labour Organisation (set up also as an intrinsic part of the same Treaty of Versailles) revolutionized working conditions for millions of workers across the planet, and I.L.O. still retains its place at the head of the U.N. agencies.

Even the difficult area of territorial conflicts marked up a surprising number of triumphs. The League stopped a dozen small wars and adjusted a vast range of international problems stretching from the notorious Polish Corridor to the disputed swamplands of Chaco between Bolivia and Paraguay. Then, there was the World Court (on which a U.S. judge sat) which settled over thirty knotty legal disputes — not one of its judgments being rejected — and built a whole new code of international law.

*   *   *   *   *

The truth is that the League was not only a Great Experiment, as it was frequently called, but a revolutionary enterprise on the world level challenging the statesmanship of some of the most enlightened personalities of the first half of this century. For the first time, a global institution whose charter —. the League Covenant — discriminated against no nation or race or ideology, brought together a new breed of practical men to actualise the poet's impossible dream: a warless world. Although they failed in their first attempt, the legacy of achievement they left behind them was no mean contribution to the human future.

They were big men. To begin with, there was Woodrow Wilson, who had thought out the original plan of a world society of independent nations. But while he saw the new order afar off, neither he nor his nation entered the promised land. That story is itself worth recalling. There was Fridtjof Nansen of Norway, indomitable Polar explorer and brilliant oceanographer, who became the saviour of millions of uprooted refugees. There was Aristide Briand of France who brought to the League his Grand Design of a European Union. There was Lord Robert Cecil, who inspired the International Peace Ballot of the 1930's to re-vivify the League.

There was also General Jan Smuts of South Africa and Wellington Koo of China and a score of leading statesmen from India and Asia and South America who brought their great talents together in the world's first Parliament of Man. Not least, for the first time, a permanent international civil service was created, under Sir Eric Drummond, which worked out the techniques for serving with integrity and impartiality the whole human race, instead of one country.

All this brings up many points of likeness with and contrasts to the United Nations. To re-discover the League today reminds us of Santayana's aphorism: "Those who do not learn the lessons of history, will live to repeat its mistakes."

When the League handed over its residuary functions to the U.N. in 1946, it passed on an indefinable something called the 'Spirit of Geneva'. This writer, who was educated in Geneva between the two Wars, knows something of what that Spirit meant for his generation. He knows that, though much was lost, much more remains to guide and encourage a new generation to carry forward the League's high ideals and actual achievements into a new age.

The author was present when Stresemann of Germany clasped the hand of Briand of France at the rostrum of the Fourth Annual Assembly and pre-Hitler Germany was admitted to the League. He was present when Arthur Henderson of Britain opened the First World Disarmament Conference and when Baron Aloisi of Italy stalked defiantly from the Council debate which had called for sanctions against Italy.

The League's two decades were busy years, full of hopes and disappointments, of innovations and surprises, of promises and compromises. They were, perhaps, the most important twenty years of this century. Did its builders build better than they knew? Were the League's shortcomings due to weaknesses within, or were the major problems kept outside it? Would it have done better if the United States had belonged? Was the League tried and found wanting, or found difficult and not tried?

To a younger generation of students, the story of these twenty turbulent years, *told from the League point of view,* may well come as quite a revelation. The obvious lessons that this First Parliament of Man had to teach the world's leaders cannot be hidden.

But are the lessons it taught being applied today? Or are we subject to the same narrow nationalisms, the same rival militarisms, the same selfish policies, and the same neurotic mentalities that conspired to bring about the League's downfall? Can the spirit of man still rise like a Phoenix from the ashes of Hamburg and Hiroshima, where the League perished, to create a warless world in the Spirit of Geneva?

Geneva   *James Avery Joyce*
1 January, 1978

PART I

YEARS OF HOPE

(1918-1920)

CHAPTER 1

The Foundling

All was illusion. Wilson failed miserably, as we all know;
his modest successes were rejected by his own Government. The ruthless men of power without vision — Lloyd
George and Clemenceau — won, and won so handsomely
that they created a legacy of hate and conflict that was to
tear Europe in pieces in the next generation.
— *Professor J. H. Plumb, Cambridge historian*

One fascination of studying the League, from its foundation
in 1919 until its floundering in 1939, lies in following the ideas
and achievements, the frustrations and disappointments of the
few enlightened statesmen, and those valiant souls who backed
them, who aimed to build for the first time a world-based
structure of many nations dedicated to the 'peace and security'
of all — a sort of embryo World Parliament.

This chapter must take us back, however, to some of the un-
palatable realities behind the 1919 settlement. For the so-called
'settlement' received this description in contrast to the unsettle-
ment that preceded and occasioned it. 'When we speak of the
necessity of an absolutely clean state and the League starting
encumbered by no disastrous heritage from the past,' said one
of the League's strongest advocates in 1919, 'we are talking
mere moonshine. You cannot ever in human affairs have a
clean slate. The work of the League will be to make the slate
gradually cleaner.' [1]

---

[1] Gilbert Murray, Professor oɪ Greek Studies at Oxford University, one-
time League delegate and Chairman of the League of Nations Union in
Britain.

What went before

That the League was born in great hope and high expectation was widely apparent at its beginning, inspite of misgivings from some of its most ardent backers. Faith in the League was a natural and popular reaction from the shattering events of 1914-1918. For nearly five years the common peoples had suffered and bled, as Europe was torn asunder and many of its cities blown to pieces. Over twelve million combat soldiers died as a result of the pre-war 'system' — or lack of system — that the peacemakers in Paris were determined to abolish and replace by the League system.

What *was* this discredited old order? The diplomatic chaos that existed in Europe in the latter part of the nineteenth century and the early years of the twentieth century must first by reviewed to understand why this terrible conflict happened at all. Such a backward glance is also necessary to follow the events that stemmed from 'The Peace that Failed'. This carry-over from the pre-war world dogged the League's footsteps from the start. "Whatever future historians may finally decide about the notorious war-guilt question, which so dangerously continues to poison the international atmosphere even today, one thing is certain," said the Swiss diplomat and scholar, Professor William E. Rappard, in 1931: "the real culprit, whose historic responsibility will always overshadow the vanity, the stupidity, and the wickedness of individual statesmen, is the pre-war system of international relations."[2]

Two important trends marked the European scene prior to 1914. One was the elaborate system of alliances that dragged nation after nation into the War, as soon as the spark was ignited in some remote spot. This international anarchy led to an arms race of unprecedented proportions. The British statesman who was Foreign Secretary in 1914 stated the obvious truth thus:

> If there are armaments on one side, there must be armaments on the other side . . . Every measure taken by one nation is noted, and leads to counter-measures by others.

---

[2] W. E. Rappard: *The Geneva Experiment* (Oxford), 1931.

The enormous growth of armaments in Europe, the sense
of insecurity and fear caused by them — it was these that
made war inevitable.[3]

This hodgepodge of self-defeating alliances had steadily
emerged since 1879. How was this? Let us try to simplify the
complicated diplomatic picture at the end of the 19th century.
After defeating the French in 1871 and creating a united Germany, Bismarck was determined to keep France without allies,
thus to protect himself from any war of revenge. A Dual
Alliance was formed between Germany and Austria-Hungary
in 1879. At the same time a treaty was made with Russia to
make it less likely that Germany would be attacked from the
East. In 1882, Italy joined this alliance, which now became the
Triple Alliance.

By these protective actions, however, Germany had forced
both France and Russia to seek one another's friendship. As a
result they formed their own alliance in 1894 — to protect each
other against the Triple Alliance. This meant that if Germany
quarrelled with France over Alsace-Lorraine, she would also
have to fight Russia; if she quarrelled with Russia over the
Balkans, she would also have to fight France.

War pacts breed more war pacts. (They still do.) England
signed the *Entente Cordiale* with France in 1904, and an
entente (understanding) with Russia in 1907. By these ententes
Britain did not exactly commit herself to war, though France
and Russia came to expect that she would fight with them,
especially following a naval agreement in 1912.

In theory, this kind of balance of power may seem plausible,
but in practice two armed bodies stand poised, ever ready to
overtopple the 'balance'. Thus, two hostile alliances were
armed and prepared to fight each other some years before
1914. No third party or mediation machinery stood between
them to take off the pressure. It was a question of luck, or
accident, as to when and where the appropriate button would
be pushed. The shadowy Concert of Europe, which had been
formed at the Congress of Vienna in 1815, lingered on,

---

[3] Lord Grey in his memoirs *Twenty-Five Years,* Vol. I (World Co.) 1926.

nebulous and unorganised. There were no rules governing the occasional meetings of ministers or on how to carry out any collective decisions. Smaller states, also, occasionally took part in major discussions; sometimes the Big Powers required them to obey their decisions, sometimes they 'protected' them.

Not until the Hague Conferences of 1899 and 1907 did the legendary Concert concern itself with humanitarian considerations and make an attempt to put restrictions on the making of war, as weapons grew more numerous and more destructive. These two Conferences initiated the drafting of conventions codifying the 'rights and duties' of belligerents and neutrals. It was a brave beginning of the rule of law in world affairs.

The first Hague Conference in 1899 was called at the suggestion of Czar Nicolas II. It brought together the United States, Japan, Mexico, Persia and Siam, as well as the European States. An international tribunal was formed, which later became the Permanent Court of Arbitration, to which nations could volunteer to take disputes for peaceful settlement. This was one short but significant step towards true international co-operation.

The second Hague Conference of 1907 was attended by 44 States, including 17 South American States, and began work on international laws restricting certain types and methods of war. A third Conference was planned to be held in 1914 — but never was. These conferences, like the Concert of Europe, were really an intensive use of the traditional methods of diplomacy. At best, they paved a little of the way for the League of Nations.

The 1914 breakdown

Against the double chain-reaction of armed alliances, we must evaluate the League's aims and objectives after the 1914-18 War. No-one can understand the League without reference to this earlier sequence of events. The spark which had ignited the conflagration was a single murder. It came when the Austrian Crown Prince Ferdinand was assassinated at

Sarajevo in Bosnia-Herzegovina by a disgruntled Serb on June 28, 1914. Bosnia was at the time Austrian territory, having been annexed in 1910. On July 23 Austria delivered an ultimatum to Serbia, demanding acceptance within 48 hours. But Austria rejected Serbia's conciliatory reply and declared war on Serbia on July 30, 1914. A week later the whole of Europe was up in arms. The pacts and counter-pacts saw to the rest.

Russia, with fears and ambitions of her own, had mobilised to support Serbia. Germany in support of Austria, demanded that Russia should demobilise and at the same time give her an assurance of neutrality. But when Serbia and Russia refused to budge from their positions, Germany declared war on both of them on August 1. On August 3 Germany declared war on France, which had already mobilised in support of her entente ally Russia.

Britain's position was at first ambiguous. Only limited help could be given to France; but the German invasion of Belgium, who called for help against the invaders, gave Britain a legal and moral case for joining in. The German Government anticipated this outcome of invading Belgium, but they had expected to knock out France quickly before turning on Russia.

According to some historians, Austria was the main war criminal, with Germany and Russia not far behind. But, in fact, few governments were blameless for their part in the escalation process. The rival alliances and national ambitions had long set the stage. The United States came in as an 'associated power' only in 1917, as a direct result of Germany's submarine campaign against merchant ships. Yet her entry was vital for the success of the Allies; and it nicely balanced the Russian withdrawal that same year when the Bolsheviks took Russia out of the war and admitted defeat by the Germans.

At the start of the war most of the governments had no convincing war or peace 'aims'. In a sense, the conflagration just happened. But during the course of the war, as the casualties and destruction worsened, ideals and objectives to justify the war and to lay down the conditions of peace were skillfully devised by the warring governments. The nations had entered the war in a state of blind emotion, even of enthusiasm; but after they were deep in mutual slaughter, as the graveyards were being filled and 'victory' seemed further and further away, war and peace 'aims' were more and more needed for popular consumption to keep the war going.

War's first victim

Did any one nation really begin the First World War? The Americans and British declared that the Germans had started the war. On the other hand, the Germans insisted that the war was on their part a 'defensive' one. Each of the countries entered the war with selfish motives, so it is difficult to determine who actually 'began' it. One significant factor behind the British declaration was undoubtedly trade rivalry. But most Western historians seem to agree that it was a war of aggression on the part of Germany. The term 'aggression' now assumes a leading role in international polemics. The 1919 Peace Treaty was based entirely on the assumption that Germany was *solely* responsible and had to be punished accordingly..

Professor A. J. P. Taylor has recently summed up this ambivalent position as follows: 'Did Germany's rulers deliberately launch a European ear, either from apprehension or to establish their domination over the Continent? The answers by historians have gone up and down with the years. Immediately after the outbreak of war, *Entente* historians usually declared that Germany had followed a course of planned aggression, while German historians claimed that she acted in self-defence. Between the wars, most historians came to agree that *the war had started by mistake.* Now we seem back at the view that German militarism was mainly responsible.'[4]

We can however be certain that both sides distorted the truth to get their public to accept what they were doing. The first victim of all war is truth. These distortions were responsible for the one-sided decisions of the victors following the war's con-

---

[4] A. J. P. Taylor: *From Sarajevo to Potsdam* (Harcourt, Brace & World) 1966.

clusion. The peace was imposed, not negotiated. In 1919, it was the war that made the peace; it was *that* sort of peace.

The conduct of the war had been quite unrestrained. It was a massacre on land. The generals for the most part made their own decisions; governmental leaders, on all sides, could rarely check them once war had begun. Both military men and their civilian masters showed an increasing disregard for human life — though in their memoirs for years afterwards they all had excellent reasons for what they did. The introduction of poisonous gases — among other things — was responsible for countless deaths and the wrecked human beings who reached their homes alive. The twelve million combatants who perished included some of the finest men of their generation, volunteers. The world was so much the poorer for their loss that the period between the two wars was left — it has been said — with the mediocre political leaders from which it suffered.

Yet it is fair to ask whether the horrors of trench warfare in 1914-18 could be blamed wholly on the generals' callousness or whether the military men were rather scapegoats for the governments and those who backed them at home? Were not the generals servants of war policies determined by both politicians and public opinion? The common people went war-mad and demanded victory at any cost. The leaders were well aware of the frightful cost of the war; yet there was no overwhelming popular demand anywhere for peace. Several opportunities presented themselves to Lloyd George, the British Prime Minister, to enter peace negotiations; but he chose instead to wage war to the finish. Was it not, in the last resort, the families and friends of the men in the trenches who drove them into battle?

Adding to the frightful massacre on land, the sea war played a decisive role in the outcome. The blockade of Germany by Britain was deliberately aimed to starve out the civilian population. This led to stronger German reliance on its submarine fleet. In 1917, they sunk the *Lusitania,* with a heavy loss of American lives, thus providing the immediate pretext for bringing the United States into the war. The following year, in November, 1918, the war finished. It left the whole of

Europe in physical ruin and moral chaos. A leading allied soldier, General J. C. Smuts of South Africa, declared:

> There are only two ways in the world: the way of force and the way of understanding. We have proved the way of force to the utmost, and seen it reduce the world to a mass of ruin.

This was the actual situation into which the League of Nations moved just one year later — abandoned from the start by the United States, the only country that had survived the war without visible destruction or economic loss or political collapse.

Meantime, the Russian Revolution had begun early in 1917 and a separate peace was made with Germany by the Bolsheviks. Before the war had ended in the West, therefore, Russia was in a state of disintegration. But from 1917 to 1922 Russia was also an occupied land — this time by the Allies! Russia's war-torn economy was in shambles. Yet at this formative stage in Russia's revolution, with social democrats in the ascendant, what was known later on as the Cold War was begun *by the West*. British and American and other Allied forces were killing Russians on their own soil in a futile attempt to put an end to the Bolshevik regime — something we easily forget, but what the Russians never forget.

In the midst of the disasters of their lost war and the unexpected allied invasion, Lenin's Bolshevik regime emerged and undertook to create out of the wreckage of the defeated Russian Empire a pilot Marxist state. Capitalism was officially abolished; all industry and commerce were placed under the management of committees (soviets) of workers, responsible to Communist-party commissars. The land, far from being distributed to the peasants (as the latter had been led to believe) was nationalized and turned over to the management of local peasant committees, who distributed it to individual peasants to be worked with their own labour. For good or ill, the Communist World had been born in pain and travail. This also was part of the League inheritance; yet we shall note in later chapters that it was not Soviet Russia which brought calamity upon the League, but Britain's allies.

Penalties of defeat

One problem that always arises with a peace settlement arose with this one. If we're going to make peace, with whom shall we make it? (The Second World War does not even yet have a formal peace treaty to *conclude* it in Europe.*) President Wilson's famous Fourteen Points, announced in February, 1918, after the United States had joined the Allies, had opened a door to conciliation with the common enemy on the basis of reason and justice for all. General Ludendorf and his fellow German generals had imagined that they would get the best deal if they agreed to a peace treaty quickly. So in November, 1918, the fighting stopped and an Armistice was proclaimed. As military men they considered it of utmost importance to retain as much of their military strength as possible, without further retreat or defeat. But they were to be sadly disillusioned.

The Peace Treaty was drawn up in Paris during the winter months and signed in June, 1919, in the Hall of Mirrors, Versailles, where many of the 18th century mirrors gave a somewhat distorted image of reality. The Germans had to deal with Clemenceau (the Tiger) of France and Lloyd George (the Welsh Wizard) of Great Britain. Woodrow Wilson was present, however, as the dominating influence. It was Wilson who had really brought the war to an end by submitting his Fourteen Points to the world's conscience as a basis of a just settlement. He realized at Versailles that many of these points had already been abrogated. But he maintained that the inclusion of a League of Nations 'covenant', as an integral chapter of the Treaty, would help in time to put right the inequities of its other provisions.

Relying on Wilson's earlier counsels of moderation, the Germans were hit by the Treaty harder then they had expected. In England, for example, strong opposition to Germany continued after the fighting stopped. The Conservatives especially insisted on a hard peace; they pressured Prime Minister Lloyd

* The Helsinki Agreement in 1975 was an informal pact to let things stay as they were, but it was not a peace treaty.

George so that he pushed through harsh terms for the Germans.

TRAITÉ DE PAIX

ENTRE LES PUISSANCES ALLIÉES ET ASSOCIÉES

ET L'ALLEMAGNE

ET PROTOCOLE

SIGNÉS À VERSAILLES, LE 28 JUIN 1919

TREATY OF PEACE

BETWEEN THE ALLIED AND ASSOCIATED POWERS

AND GERMANY

AND PROTOCOL

SIGNED AT VERSAILLES, JUNE 28, 1919

This is not the place to analyse the Treaty in detail. For one thing, the Treaty imposed impossible reparation payments against the Germans — a subject we take up in Chapter 6. These had to be whittled down later; but not before they had become a major argument for Hitler's campaign of revenge. Most of the German fleet and submarines were ordered to be sunk, and they were. Battleships were intended for sale as scrap iron, but were scuttled by the Germans first. Germany lost all her colonies in Africa and China, plus the rich Alsace-Lorraine area to France and some border provinces to Belgium. The Kaiser was indicted in the Treaty to be put on trial; but he preferred to reside in Holland until his death, and so escaped trial.

Clemenceau gained the best deal for France. The French received back Alsace-Lorraine, and also gained military hegemony in Europe temporarily. Germany had been an hereditary enemy of France for ages, but France got the power it needed by the Treaty. 'As for Clemenceau, uninterested as he

Lloyd George, Clemenceau and Wilson strolling in Paris

was in geographical detail,' stated a leading American expert at the Conference, Charles Seymour, 'there was no-one who perceived more clearly the relations of geography and political power in their larger strategic aspects. The essence of his policy concerned the defence of France. For her protection from the assault of a revivified Germany he recognized two key positions: first, a demilitarized Rhineland on the German western frontier; second, a fortified bastion in Bohemia under Czechoslovakia as an ally of France. "He who holds Bohemia controls Central Europe".'[5] The Tiger got his way. But Britain spent the next two decades trying to assure France that Germany would not hit back again — all in vain!

The victors also insisted that Germany had to become democratic, which was quite a switch from a virtual military dictatorship. The post-war civilian and republican government and the new federal constitution, drawn up by dedicated and liberal-minded leaders, became known as the Weimar Republic. But they had to start their short-lived democracy with too many disabilities to last long. They had lost much valuable territory and physical assets; impossible financial obligations had been placed upon them by the Treaty. Nor were they admitted to the League until 1926, as we shall recall in Chapter 5. No democracy could survive for long under such exactions and impositions from without.

A modern historian of Germany has pointed out, moreover, that a large part of the tragedy of Germany had been due to the fact that the civil government of the old empire had fallen increasingly under military control. It was a condition which continued and led directly to the eventual rise of Hitler.[6]

War to end war?

The British blockade against Germany continued for two years after the fighting had officially ended in 1918. Thousands of ordinary citizens were still dying of starvation under the imposed 'peace'. The beginnings of the Nazi movement can be

[5] Quoted in I. J. Lederer: *The Versailles Settlement* (Heath) 1966.
[6] Richard M. Watt: *The Kings Depart* (Simon and Schuster) 1969.

readily traced back to this turbulent time. The common people had nothing to fall back on, nothing to hope for. Hitler later spoke of the 'diktat of Versailles'. The Germans knew exactly what he meant. The awful defeat, the continued war conditions, the hunger, the raging epidemics: all ensured a wretched start for the Weimar Republic, which it was hoped would be one of the foundation stones of a new Europe. It collapsed within a decade, in spite of courageous statesmen like Gustav Stresemann, who struggled to save it. That was the end of 'democracy' in Germany.

War and democracy never make easy bedfellows. This was well brought out by another contemporary historian, Hajo Holborn, as follows:

> In 1919 no autocratic or authoritarian power could obstruct the peace settlement, and peace-making was the exclusive responsibility of the democratic nations ... 'the war to end war' turned out to be the harbinger of even greater disaster.[7]

Public opinion among the victors tied the hands of the statesmen at Versailles. Wilson often found himself alone in seeking not a peace of vengeance, but a peace of justice. 'The peoples of England and France were in a mood to "hang the Kaiser" and to "squeeze the orange until the pips squeak". An hysterical populace in the Allied countries called for the punishment and destruction of Germany. Allied leaders, true to the principles of democracy, bowed to the storm.'[8]

To the East, Russia lost about one third of its territory under the Treaty. The Peace Conference set up Estonia, Latvia, and Lithuania as independent sovereign states, cut out from former Czarist Russia. Poland was resurrected and Yugoslavia was formed from Serbia and other Balkan countries. The Austro-Hungarian Empire was broken up by the Treaty and Hungary lost much of its territory. Ex-enemy Bulgaria shrunk to about a third of its size after the war, while friendly Greece gained a little more land. Rumania and Poland benefited most of all. Of all these alleged democracies thus set up, Czechoslovakia was

---

[7] Hajo Holborn in I. J. Lederer, *op. cit.*
[8] Paul Birdsall: *Versailles, Twenty Years After* (Allen & Unwin) 1941.

the only successful one, largely due to its brilliant post-war leadership under Masaryk. Yet even Czechoslovakia survived for less than twenty years as a viable state.

'Every government,' to quote Charles Seymour again, who was a close associate of Colonel House at the Conference, 'felt that justice to its own people demanded a protection of national security; and this protection frequently could be achieved only at the expense of another people.' This common dilemma was enshrined in the opening words of Wilson's 14th point calling for 'a general association of nations' and yet clashed throughout the Conference with his concluding words upholding 'political independence and territorial integrity of great and small states alike'.

The Polish Corridor gave Poland access to the sea; but to do this it split Germany in two. Danzig on the coast was made a free port and put under the supervision of the League of Nations. One of the most onerous and thankless tasks of the League of Nations was to protect such minorities. It was hoped that this particular amputation could be healed with time. It wasn't. The Germans were finally "reunited" when, in 1938, Austria was invaded and became part of the German Reich. Northwestern Czechoslovakia, the Sudetenland, soon followed. So did the Second World War. When Hitler attacked in 1939, he attacked eastwards — through Poland.

Where lies justice?

No telescoped account of the effects of the Treaty can portray all the factors involved. A plethora of books has appeared in many languages analysing the pros and cons, depending on each author's point of view. But no normal brain can deny today that iron chain of causation which ran from the treaty of 1919 to the tragedy of 1939. Yet many mighty voices praised the Treaty and spoke confidently of 'peace in our time'. For example, one of its beneficiaries, Thomas Masaryk — shortly to become the first President of Czechoslovakia — declared that "the Peace Treaties have created juster conditions throughout Europe, and we are entitled to expect that

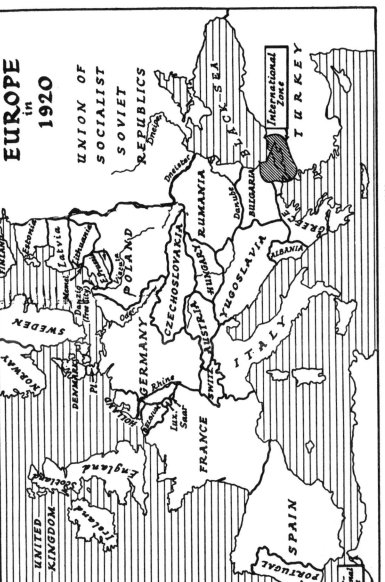

Europe re-carved by the Paris Peace Settlement in 1919

the tension between States and races will decrease." Masaryk was a wise man, but no judgment could have been more mistaken.

A similar optimistic interpretation by a more recent apologist of the Treaty can be taken as typical of many others: 'The cause both of peace and justice was served in eastern Europe by the treaties; and better served than they had been for centuries. It was not the Versailles system, but the success of the Germans in wrecking it in 1938 and 1939 that caused the Second World War. The real German grievance against the settlement was not that it was a diktat or that they had been cheated by President Wilson. It was chiefly that it prevented them from dominating and exploiting the valleys of the Vistula and the Danube and kept them away from the approach to Asia Minor and the Ukraine, and because it emphatically asserted that in south-eastern Europe the Slavs had as much right to an independent existence as the Germans and Magyars.'[9]

A foremost British diplomat, who was present at Paris, Harold Nicolson, summed up his own opinion as follows: 'The historian, with every justification, will come to the conclusion that we were very stupid men . . . We arrived determined that a peace of justice and wisdom should be negotiated: we left it conscious that the treaties imposed upon our enemies were neither just nor wise . . .'[10]

The Wilsonian settlement

Against this sombre background, no-one can discredit the blessed and courageous role played by President Woodrow Wilson in stopping the war in 1918 and getting the Peace Conference on its feet in 1919. Hajo Holborn has thus summed up Wilson's bid for popular acclaim: 'Wilson's program appealed to the common man, and the popular ovations that he received everywhere he went in Europe were genuine. To almost everybody it seemed that the program offered a way to end the cruel

[9] L. C. B. Seaman: *From Vienna to Versailles* (Harper & Row) 1955.
[10] Harold Nicolson: *Peacemaking 1919* (Harcourt, Brace) 1939.

ENREGISTREMENT DES TRAITÉS
REGISTRATION OF TREATIES.

According to Article XVIII of the Covenant "every treaty or international engagement entered into . . . by any member of the League shall be forthwith registered with the Secretariat . . . No such treaty or international engagement shall be binding until so registered." This is exactly the position today under the United Nations.

bloodshed and to cure the wounds that four years of war had inflicted on all national societies.'[11]

Unquestionably the chief architect of the League of Nations, other statesmen of world rank helped Wilson from behind the scenes, such as Lord Robert Cecil and General Jan Smuts. A close colleague, Ray Stannard Baker, has drawn this heroic picture of the doughty champion in the midst of battle: 'No-one who really saw the President in action at Paris, saw what he had to do after he came home from Europe in meeting the great new problems which grew out of the war — will for a moment belittle the immensity of his task, or underrate his extra-ordinary endurance, energy, and courage.'

Yet while Wilson was regarded as a *deus ex machina* in Europe, this was not the view in the United States. Wilson was fully aware that the opposition senators would not ratify the League Covenant without a great deal of pressure. But he still believed they would accept it as a provision of the Treaty. His own judgment faltered. Viscount Bryce, the brilliant scholar who had headed a distinguished committee to work on drafts of the League's Covenant, reflected the keen disappointment in Britain over Wilson's failure back home with the remark: 'As for Wilson and the United States Senate, why will he persist in stroking the cat the wrong way?'

The desperate struggle of Wilson to win his own people for his League, is part of American domestic history; but we are concerned in these pages with the international aspects. Through the implacable hostility of Henry Cabot Lodge, the Senate ultimately failed by a handful of votes to recognize the League of Nations for the sterling opportunity it offered the human race for the future of world peace. (Two years later the United States made a separate peace with Germany.) Although his own country had refused to join, and although the League failed to prevent the Second World War, we shall note in these chapters how often it served as a valuable model for the United Nations. When Wilson declared: 'I would rather lose in a cause that will one day triumph, than triumph in a cause that will one day lose,' he foresaw the rightful destiny of his own nation and

---

[11] I. J. Lederer, *op. cit.*

Wilson at his desk

assured his place in the hearts of reasonable men for all time.

The success of the League in its initial stages clearly depended on the combined and enthusiastic support of the Big Three victorious democracies — the United States, Britain, and France. The refusal of the United States to join was a body blow from which it never recovered. Britain and France also tended to lose faith in it; they began to pursue traditionally nationalistic aims and fell back on regional pacts that ultimately led, by their very nature, to war. The eminent editor of *The Papers of Woodrow Wilson* came to this solemn conclusion: 'The great tragedy of the post-war period was not that the Versailles Treaty was imperfect. It was that the forces of reconciliation could not operate rapidly enough without American leadership in the League, that France and Great Britain had neither the will nor the strength to defend the treaty alone during the 1930's and, above all, that the German people submitted to demonic forces that promised a speedy rectification of all the injustices of Versailles.' [12]

[12] Arthur S. Link: *Woodrow Wilson, A Profile* (Hill & Wang) 1968.

Facing the realities

Soon after the peace settlement had been signed, the victorious nations were again bickering. The Cold War over Communism had begun. A yet more devastating war was being prepared and struck again within twenty years. This time, the armed truce culminated in the atom bomb. The question has been asked: was not the League betrayed by incompetent, short-sighted and self-seeking 'realists' who gave it lip-service, but evaded or flouted its covenants? Looking back over those twenty troubled years, one might well agree with Professor Link: 'Among all the major statesmen and thoughtful critics of his age, President Wilson was in fact the supreme realist, and because this is true, what he stood for and fought to accomplish has large meaning for our own generation.'

Inspite of all, the League of Nations established its headquarters in an oversized Victorian hotel in Geneva in 1920. Around its very cradle all Europe lay exhausted in a state of frightful devastation. In addition to the war dead and mutilated, over 20 million Europeans also died of influenza that same year; the pitiful refugees and ex-prisoners of war could be counted in millions over a dozen lands. The beginning of a superhuman endeavour, it had a seemingly impossible task

Where the League began

ahead of it, with basic resources and manpower yet to be recruited. A foundling child, deserted by its foster-mother — some supremely hopeful people of goodwill still expected that all the wrongs in the Treaty would be put right by it as it grew. Yet it survived the pangs of its tortured birth for two decades. Its actual achievements, and they were many and substantial, must be measured against the hard realities of its time.

This is where the League story must begin. On April 28, 1919, the Covenant was adopted by the Peace Conference and just two months later was signed by thirty-two nations on June 28, 1919. Under the terms of the Treaty, the League of Nations itself came formally into existence on January 10, 1920.

CHAPTER 2

The New Covenant

"What we seek is the reign of law
based on the consent of the
governed and sustained by the
organised opinion of mankind."

— *Woodrow Wilson*

It is astonishing that, considering its origins, the Covenant
should have become the short and simple document it turned
out to be. From the point of view of terminology, its clarity is
indeed praiseworthy. But a reading of the text can give little
cause for enthusiasm. It makes mundane reading when compared with other historical documents. It lacks the sonorous
clauses of the English Magna Carta or of the U.S. Declaration
of Independence. Nor does it match the polished literary grace
of the Charter of the United Nations.

Not only were the drafting difficulties enormous, as noted in
Chapter 1, but the reprehensible tradition of drafting treaties
so as to leave as many loopholes as possible (through which the
parties might escape later on) had not been ignored at Versailles. Some of these gaps — deliberate or accidental — we
shall meet with in later chapters, when we seek to follow how
the fundamental law of the League was applied to concrete
situations. What is attempted here is an all-round picture of
what the Covenant set out to do and what its limitations were.
It is important to assess the Covenant for *what it was,* rather
than what many people *expected* of it — and were gravely disappointed in the event.

THE NEW COVENANT 43

An outstanding League authority and British scholar, Sir Alfred Zimmern, put forward this modest claim for the League:

> The League of Nations is not a patent method of inter-state co-operation applicable to all states at any moment of history. It is a particular moment of history when there are certain principal powers with clearly marked characteristics and policies.[1]

The Covenant is not strictly a *legal* document at all. It is not written in legal language. President Wilson himself never intended to create a formal constitution for the world. His whole approach was pragmatic. He wanted an organisation to be set up 'in general form and agreed to and *set in motion*'. Experience was to 'guide subsequent action'. He looked for an association of states that worked, and that worked to keep the world's peace.

Even a formal constitution, drawn with the utmost regard for strict rules, is subject as time goes on to interpretations of its language, which adapt it to the changing needs of the society by which it was established. That famous American, Justice Holmes, has pointed out that 'when we are dealing with words that are also a constituent act, like the Constitution of the United States, we must realise that they have called into life a being the development of which could not have been foreseen clearly by the most gifted of its begetters.'[2]

This was even more true of the Covenant. As one of its drafters, M. Clemenceau, declared: 'Its articles are not subject to a narrow and technical construction.' During one of the later League debates another French statesman, Aristide Briand, similarly remarked: 'The best thing to be done with legal arguments in our meetings is to put them to bed in the soothing hospitality of a comfortable pigeon-hole and bring them out as little as possible from their repose.' (How very different is all this from debates at the United Nations today,

---

[1] Alfred Zimmern: *The League of Nations and the Rule of Law* (Macmillan) 1936.
[2] *Missouri v. Holland* (1920), 252 U.S. 416.

where every word of the Charter is carefully argued and weighed!)

The title of the Covenant itself is distinctly Anglo-American. Both the words Covenant and League take us, in fact, back to the 17th century's constitutional struggles. The opening text states simply that 'The high Contracting Parties . . . agree to this Covenant of the League of Nations.' By this agreement the contract was made and the League was created.

The word Covenant recalls the Solemn League and Covenant of 1643. It also takes us back to the acts by which the earlier British immigrants to America 'combined themselves into a body politic for the purpose of making equal laws for the general good,' as John Marshall once put it. The word Covenant had drawn special meaning for the Puritans from the Old Testament, where we find such terms as: 'Look upon the covenant; for all the earth is full of darkness and cruel habitations' (74th Psalm, v. 21). President Wilson must have looked back with special pride to his Presbyterian ancestry when he thus chose for the League a symbolic title and enshrined its living embodiment in the Covenant.

Drafting the Covenant

It must not be assumed, however, that the Covenant owed everything to Woodrow Wilson. Far from it. Its very matter-of-fact terminology was testimony to an ample British draftsmanship. From the first weeks of the war in 1914 various voluntary groups in the warring countries began to produce manifestos on 'war aims' and schemes for post-war settlement — though the belligerent governments were slow to commit themselves.

The actual name League of Nations was coined by an Oxford professor, Goldsworthy Lowes Dickinson, who helped to found the League of Nations Society in 1915. Two months later the League to Enforce Peace was founded in Independence Hall, Philadelphia, with former President William Howard Taft as president. A League of Free Nations Association was also formed in New York City by leading lawyers and scholars; while in London British liberals and socialists set up the Union of Democratic Control to further the establishment of an international organisation to keep the peace. Similar citizen groups were at work in other countries, including Germany and Austria-Hungary.

It was not until early in 1918, however, that steps were taken by the British Government to explore the possibilities of a League. The Foreign Secretary, Lord Balfour, on the initiative of Lord Robert Cecil, appointed a Committee 'to inquire into the various schemes for establishing peace by means of settling international disputes.' Lord Phillimore became chairman and the official Report became known by his name; its members were three leading historians and three senior members of the Foreign Office. The Phillimore Report did not visualize a permanent organisation like the League actually became, but proposed a body which could be called into immediate existence if war threatened. This body was to be limited in the beginning to the Allies, and nothing was suggested about disarmament.

The French Government had likewise appointed a Committee to study the project of a League, with Léon Bourgeois, a former Prime Minister, as chairman. Their Report adumbrated a far more comprehensive scheme than that of the Phillimore Committee. An International Tribunal was to have full power to decide disputes and a detailed list of diplomatic and economic sanctions was included. In fact, a permanent military staff was proposed to 'investigate all military questions'. The French view was that if military sanctions were necessary, as they thought they were, then the obvious thing was to make careful preparation for them beforehand. The logic of this view was that if states knew that preparations had been made for dealing with aggression, they would be less likely to sin themselves.[3]

At the time that President Wilson made his Fourteen Points speech on January 8, 1918, he had no definite scheme in mind. The Phillimore and French Reports were sent to him,

---

[3] These and other essential documents are reproduced in David Miller: *The Drafting of the Covenant* (Putnam, New York) 1928.

In December 1918, a month after the war ended, President Wilson left New York for Europe on the George Washington

and the first American draft was drawn up by the President's chief consultant, Colonel House. Wilson then studied these documents and made his own first draft. This provided for meetings of representatives of the Powers, a permanent secretariat, guarantees of territory, disarmament and compulsory arbitration, and for organising the military forces of the states members against any member who went to war.

In November, 1918, Lord Robert Cecil took charge of the League of Nations section that had been set up at the Foreign Office. He studied the Wilson draft, and drew up a document which was known as the Cecil Draft, which became the nearest approach to an official British document. In December that year General Smuts published a widely discussed pamphlet on the future League. His authority as statesman and soldier carried great weight. Naturally interested in the former German colonies in Africa, he gave close attention to the idea of establishing Mandates under the general care of the League. He proposed a General Conference (which became the

Viscount Cecil.

Assembly) of all member states, and a Council which was to be an executive body, consisting of the Great Powers, together with representatives of smaller powers taken in rotation. He further suggested the nationalization of armament factories, because of the scandals associated with the private manufacture and trade in arms.

We need not describe the many variations and alterations which were made in these basic drafts before the League of Nations Commission was set up by the Peace Conference in Paris to formalise them, under the chairmanship of President Wilson himself in January, 1919. Sufficient is it to remark that much debate had gone on around them in the previous months. But one question of timing arises of some importance: Would it not have been better to have postponed the designing of the League's Covenant until men's minds were cooler?

Wilson was determined, as we have seen, that the League should be made an integral part of the Treaty. If a decision to set up the League had been postponed, there was grave danger that all kinds of obstacles might intervene. To Wilson the League of Nations was the paramount consideration. On his way across the Atlantic he declared frankly that 'He could not see how a treaty of peace could be drawn up or how both elasticity and security could be obtained save under a League of Nations. The opposite of such a course was to maintain the idea of the Great Powers and of a balance of power, and such an idea had always produced only aggression and war. The people are heartily sick of such a course and want the Peace Conference and the powers to take an entirely new course of action.' [4]

Yet, although the Covenant was part and parcel of the Treaty, the Covenant stood on its own feet as the sole authority for an independent organisation with its own separate life. To have kept the Covenant outside the Treaty, would have changed the character of the 1919 settlement altogether. If the Treaty had not been linked with the Covenant, it would have been a very different treaty — and probably never signed by anyone. It should not be forgotten that a state of war still existed and the blockade of Germany continued until the Treaty was actually signed and ratified. So the Treaty had to come first and come quickly. After the Treaty had been concluded, it would have been a practical impossibility to have re-assembled a world conference for negotiating an international scheme on the lines of the Covenant. President Wilson knew this danger all too well. Such a separate conference would almost certainly have suffered the same limitations as the Hague Conferences of 1899 and 1907.

As is generally known, it was ultimately a provision of the United States' constitution, requiring a two-thirds majority for the approval of a treaty by the Senate, that blocked United States acceptance of the Treaty, including the Covenant, even with some reservations. The two-thirds rule provided the enemies of Wilson with just the weapon they needed to destroy him — and his League. Had the normal democratic rule of voting by a majority applied, the Treaty would have been ratified and the United States would have become a founding member of the League.

In 1787, the U.S. Constitution itself was ratified in Massachusetts by 187 votes to 165, in Virginia by 89 votes to 79, in New York by 30 votes to 27 — all these majorities were *smaller* than the majority in the Senate which in fact failed to ratify the Covenant by 49 votes to 35. The final irony of this historic defeat and its tragic consequences for America and the world was emphasized by the fact that at the 1920 Election

---

[4] Quoted in E. E. Reynolds: *The League Experiment* (Nelson) 1938.

leading members of the Republican Party had issued a manifesto to the effect that a Republican president, if elected instead of President Wilson, could be entrusted to bring America into an 'Association of Nations' hardly distinguishable from Wilson's League.

One of those tragic consequences was summed up by a British journalist and well-known contemporary editor as follows:

> 'By no possibility could the League of Nations have been created by Europe alone. Britain and Europe together could not have brought it about. Without America it never could have been established . . . America seceded from the League. Wilson fell. With him fell half the mass of the original peace-plan . . . Externally, the forms remained almost the same at Geneva. One nation amongst so many was missing. But the nation that went out was equal in weight to any twenty or thirty of the smaller nations who form half the League.' [5]

The four pledges

The Preamble, of course, is the best guide to what the League set as its main goals. It is so brief that it can be read in half a minute. It simply states that the parties, 'in order to promote international co-operation and achieve international peace and security' have agreed under the Covenant to attain these ends by—

the acceptance of obligations not to resort to war,

the prescription of open, just and honourable relations between nations,

the firm establishment of international law as the actual rule of conduct among Governments,

the maintenance of justice and a scrupulous respect for all treaty obligations.

---

[5] J. L. Garvin: *Problems of Peace* (London) 1931.

These four pledges were given by the total of sixty-one states which became members of the League between 1919 and 1939 — ten of whom, however, left the organisation on various dates.[6] It will be the main interest of our later chapters to check the actual performance of the League members against these rather general aims and purposes.

The text of the Covenant consists of 26 articles and falls roughly into five sections. The first seven articles set out the bare constitution of the League, and these will be considered below. Then follow Articles 8 and 9, dealing with what most members considered to be of primary importance, namely, *the reduction of national armaments to the lowest point consistent with national safety*.

Articles 10 to 21 form the bulk of the Covenant. They lay down the methods by which League members proposed to handle their disputes, so as to prevent them breaking out into war. These articles tell us a good deal about the respective functions of the Assembly and the Council. Article 19 in this central section was really a revolutionary proposal; it boldly recommends the reconsideration of treaties which have been inapplicable, as well as conditions which might endanger the peace of the world. These were indeed advanced ideas at that time — had they been put into practice.

Articles 22 to 25 consisted of guidelines for improving the living conditions of mankind. The final Article 26 prescribes the rules for amending the Covenant. That, in essence, is all this revolutionary document amounted to.

It was soon found that the central group of articles, dealing with war prevention, was far from complete. So the earlier years of the League were spent — as we shall note in Part II of this book — in filling in the gaps by designing external security pacts, such as the Geneva Protocol of 1924, the Locarno Pact of 1925, and the more famous 1928 Briand-Kellogg Pact. We can compare this process with the more recent attempt to supplement the United Nations Charter by outside military alliances, such as the North Atlantic Treaty Organisation

---

[6] See list of League members accompanying full text of Covenant as Appendix 2.

(NATO) in 1949 and the now defunct South East Asia Treaty Organisation (SEATO) in 1954. If the U.N. follows the League pattern, in neither case will the outside pacts have strengthened the world organisation. On the contrary, they will have by-passed it and weakened it.[7]

Novelty of the League

The novelty of the League lay in the fact that there had never been any world body like it before; although it had gathered together a lot of ideas and practices from the recent past. Up to 1919, states alone had been considered the subjects of inter-national law. Now there existed a new kind of organisation based on international law which was certainly not a State, but was a legal entity. What, then, was the League? The Covenant clearly sets it up as an association of States, a *Société des Nations,* as the French more correctly called it. As such, it possessed rights and obligations, organs, a permanent staff, and a budget of its own. Yet it was neither a State nor a Union — that is an organisation of states in the sense that the United States or any other federal state is. Clearly it was not a super-state, with domination *over* other states. But it was assumed from the beginning that the League would be open to *all* states and eventually become a truly World Organisation.

In short, it was an Association of Nations agreeing to limit their freedom of independent action on certain points, in order 'to promote international co-operation and to achieve inter-national peace and security'. The Covenant framers had been hesitant in laying down rigidly what should or should not be done. What they desired was to bring the Members together in regular meetings to consolidate their common interests — above all, peace.

In the words of a leading British jurist: 'The League is some-thing new in international life, a new result of international necessities and the co-operation which they demand.'[8] Some of these international necessities had already taken shape as

---

[7] The defects of the present-day military alliances are dealt with in detail in the present author's *End of an Illusion* (Allen & Unwin) 1969.

[8] Sir John Fisher Williams: *Some Aspects of the Covenant* (Oxford) 1934.

functional organisations. Article 24 prescribed for them as follows: 'All such international bureaux and all commissions for the regulation of matters of international interest hereafter constituted shall be placed under the direction of the League.' The League, was, therefore, an amalgam of the old and the new.

Just as the League was different from anything in the past, so it was different from the United Nations, which took over practically all the functions of the old League. But it is significant that, when the U.N. was formed in 1945, 'the High Contracting Parties' of the Covenant became 'We, the Peoples' of the Charter.

It will also be noticed that the degree of co-operation between the League and its members was very restricted under the Covenant. The League had no power to issue anything in the nature of a command. No member could have any obligation or duty imposed on it by any organ of the League. But if any member failed to comply with its undertakings under Article 16 'not to resort to war', certain duties fell on the Council — sometimes called sanctions — which we shall describe later when dealing with specific breaches of the Covenant.

The Assembly could also *expel* members for a breach of the Covenant. But these coercive actions by the League, acting as an overall organisation, were minimal and never became in practice a real threat to the sovereignty of its members.

This emphasis on the independence or sovereignty of each member was apparent in Article 1, permitting any member to withdraw from the League, after giving two years' notice in due form — in which case the member was virtually to be the judge of its own action. Nine states did voluntarily withdraw. (No such provision for expulsion or withdrawal exists in the Charter today.) But the strongest evidence in favour of the members' sovereignty could best be seen in the unanimity rule. Article 5 provided that, except for matters of procedure, 'decisions of *any meeting* of the Assembly or of the Council shall require the agreement of all the members represented at the meeting.' So the famous veto principle, which has received so much publicity since the Second World War in respect of the U.N. Security Council, was even more stringent in the days of the League.

Protection against infringement of state sovereignty was, in fact, more rigid under the Covenant than under the Charter. Article 15 (para. 8) lays down that if a dispute arises from a matter which, under international law, is *solely* within the domestic jurisdiction of a member, the Council can take no action on it. The U.N. Charter (Article 2, para. 7) softens this restriction to 'essentially within' the domestic jurisdiction of a Member State. Human Rights, for example, are not essentially within a State Member's jurisdiction. The U.N. has, therefore, wider scope for intervention and has frequently insisted on this broader interpretation.

The Covenant also included a significant prohibition in Article 21 which ran: 'Nothing in this Covenant shall be deemed to affect the validity of international engagements, such as treaties of arbitration or regional understandings like the Monroe doctrine, for securing the maintenance of peace.' This exclusion was plainly intended as a concession to the prevailing political attitude of the U.S. Senate — but to no avail. (The U.N. Charter contains Article 103 which *over-rules* all inconsistent treaty obligations in favour of the Charter.)

The assumption of the Covenant was, as we have said, that the League was to become a universal organisation. But it was also the assumption that the League would be composed only of free — that is to say 'self-governing' — nations. No particular form of free government was, however, laid down in the Covenant, whether monarchical or republican. The modern type of totalitarian state had not then come into the picture.

Woodrow Wilson's own concept of a new era of international democracy was evident throughout the Covenant. The other Western members had no quarrel with this concept. This meant that all members had to be *equal* in their sovereignty rights. Yet at the same time, Wilson looked to the League system to protect the weaker nations against the stronger. Speaking in Paris in April, 1919, he said:

Nobody can read anything connected with its institution or read any of the Articles in the Covenant itself without realising that it is an attempt — the first serious and systematic attempt made in the world — to put nations on a footing of equality with each other in their international relations . . . and to secure for those nations which could not successfully protect themselves, if attacked by the stronger nations of the world, the support of strong nations of the world in their defence.

The sinews of peace

Coming now to the internal structure of the League the following diagram gives at a glance the relations of its various organs:—

The League of Nations: Its three sections

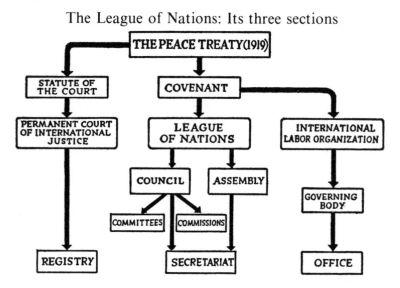

Leaving aside the two outside 'wings', the World Court and the International Labour Office, for treatment in later chapters, we note that the two main governing organs of the League are the Assembly and the Council. In spite of the stress we had laid on independence and sovereignty, the Spirit of Geneva did help to cement together, as it developed, many of the nationalistic viewpoints. Meeting year by year, the delegates came to have an understanding of each other's problems. More than one delegate expressed it thus: 'Before I came to Geneva, I always voted for what I thought best for my own nation; but now I try to vote for what is best for mankind — since I realise that that will be best for my own nation in the end!'

Another famous statesman who served the League, Salvador de Madariaga, once said: 'Yet while, indeed, the Covenant may be compared to a limited contract between sovereignties for limited co-operation in limited conditions for limited aims, the spirit of the world community which prompted it was so strong that world public opinion, and even statesmen, have expected of the Covenant more than it could give, and have thought it was more than it actually was.' [9]

THE ASSEMBLY met at least once a year. It consisted of three delegates from each member nation, but each delegation had only *one vote*. These annual Assemblies became more and more important as time went on. Prime Ministers and other heads of governments, foreign ministers and secretaries of state began to attend as a matter of habit. French and English were the official languages; though any other language could be used, if the speaker brought his interpreter along.

The Assembly could deal with any matters 'within the sphere of action of the League or affecting the peace of the world.' Its special functions included the selection (to begin with) of the four lesser Powers who were to be elected on the Council; the admission of new Members; reconsideration of obsolete treaties; and consideration with the Council of amendments to the Covenant. Not least, in the matter of disputes — as will be seen later — the parties could elect to have their cases determined by the Assembly. In fact, the growing influence of the Assembly was demonstrated by the changes which took place in its composition over the years. More and more first ministers came regularly to Geneva. For example, during its first decade the number of Prime Ministers and Foreign Secretaries who attended its annual sessions rose steadily from six to twenty-nine.

---

[9] Salvador de Madariaga: *The World's Design* (Allen & Unwin) 1938.

"The Assembly met once a year"

There were three reasons for what Professor Rappard calls 'the decisive influence in the establishment and consolidation of the Assembly's unexpected preponderance.' First, it was decided in 1920 that the Assembly was to meet annually, although the Covenant had provided only for meetings 'at stated intervals and from time to time as occasion may require.' As a result of this decision the whole life of the League pivoted on the September meetings of the Assembly. Around this annual event the Council and the other League bodies organized their activity, based on a yearly review prepared by the Secretary-General. Secondly, the financial existence of the League rested on an annual budget approved by the Assembly. The third reason for the Assembly's importance lay in the publicity of its debates. By thus allowing public opinion, through the press and, later on, direct radio reports, to follow and almost to participate in its discussions, the Assembly soon identified itself with the contemporary world.[10]

---

[10] W. E. Rappard: *The Geneva Experiment* (Oxford) 1931.

Journalists flocked to Geneva and gave the Assemblies worldwide publicity. Although the delegates spoke for their own nations, a few of them — like Dr. Fridtjof Nansen of Norway or Aristide Briand or Lord Robert Cecil — became world figures. They began to speak for civilisation as a whole. This was the beginning of a favourable world opinion, without which neither the League nor its successor — the U.N. — could hope to survive. As Professor Gilbert Murray, the British classical scholar who became one of its leading spokesmen in the English-speaking world, stated when the League began in 1920:

> The League has got to redeem the world, and naturally it starts with a world badly in need of redemption. It is the men and women of goodwill in all nations who must provide the force and the direction. The League itself is only an emblem and an instrument.[11]

The League did, in fact, make a complete break with the past in a new kind of relationship between an official body of diplomats and public opinion. The guiding principle of the new organisation was to give the widest publicity to its activities, so publicity became an inseparable element of the League's action. "Though Wilson's demand for 'open covenants, openly arrived at' was never fully implemented, more delicate and more controversial questions were discussed in public at Geneva than anywhere else in the world. League meetings were public as a rule and secrecy was the exception."[12]

The League even worked out a number of detailed measures to be taken in time of emergency, including a special aeroplane and motor service. Since 1932, the League had its own radio at Prangins, close to Geneva, powerful enough to maintain communication as far as Argentina, China, and Australia. In an international crisis the League, with a Swiss observer, had complete control of this means of broadcasting the facts of the situation. It was used several times in the crises described in Chapter 7.

---

[11] Gilbert Murray: *The Covenant Explained* (London) 1920.

[12] E. F. Ranshofen-Wertheimer: *The International Secretariat* (Carnegie) 1945.

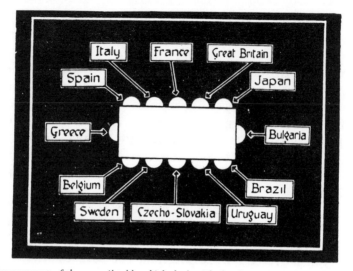

Arrangement of the council table which dealt with the dispute between Greece and Bulgaria

THE COUNCIL was a much smaller body than the Assembly and met three or four times a year. It first consisted of representatives of the BIG FOUR — the four powers that had won the war, alongside the United States — Britain, France, Italy, and Japan. Germany was admitted in 1926 and Russia in 1934. In addition, smaller nations took turns sitting on the Council, but the rules never allowed the weaker powers to outvote the big ones. In 1922 membership was raised to ten and in 1926 to fourteen to satisfy the claims of impatient candidates. But the Council was never truly the executive of the League; it was a kind of more manageable interim Assembly. The Council's decisions were mostly in the form of *recommendations.* But since the Assembly was so large a body, it was natural that the Council, in dealing with emergencies, should exercise the authority of the League. The extraordinary work that it did in keeping the peace and the way in which it handled many international disputes will be described in later chapters.

Generally speaking, the decisions of both the Assembly and the Council had to be *unanimous.* However, there were several important exceptions: for instance, admission to membership (decided by a two-thirds majority of the Assembly), questions of procedure (decided by a bare majority), and amendments to the Covenant (unanimity in the Council and a bare majority in the Assembly). For activities entrusted to the League under the Peace Treaty, a bare majority was usually sufficient.

Reverting to the foot of the diagram, one of the biggest differences between the old Concert of Europe and the new League of Nations could be seen in the setting up of a permanent staff or secretariat. They numbered over six hundred and were drawn from some fifty nationalities. They formed a splendid team, working behind the scenes of the Assembly and the Council. Their functions are sufficiently important to devote Chapter 3 mainly to them.

Coping with war

Looking again at those central articles of the Covenant, the League's panacea for coping with war can be called the Three A's — they began with Armaments, then tackled Aggression, and went on to lay down a procedure for Arbitration and other alternative means for settling disputes. Only a bare outline of these vitally important provisions can be attempted here, so as to set our later chapters within the context of the Covenant.

Under Article 8, it was the task of the Council to 'formulate plans for reducing armaments to the lowest point consistent with national safety and the enforcement by common action of international obligations.' But no obligation rested upon any State to *act* upon them. These plans for limiting armaments were to be revised at least every 10 years. All the Members of the League undertook to interchange full information as to 'the scale of their armaments, and their military, naval, and air programmes.'

Article 10 spoke of mutual guarantees against external aggression. Each member was obligated to guarantee the territory and independence of all other members against external aggression. The Council's job was to advise on *how* this obligation was to be fulfilled. The words 'external aggression' were purposely used to preclude the League from intervening if asked by a Government to help suppress a national movement within its boundaries.

Most important was Article 11. Any war whatever, or any threat of war, was henceforth to be regarded as the *concern of the whole League,* which must take the necessary steps to safeguard peace. It was the 'friendly right' of any member to draw the attention of the Assembly or Council to 'any circumstance whatever affecting international relations which threatens to disturb international peace or the good understanding between nations upon which peace depends.'

Coming to arbitration, all disputes between Members of the League had to be submitted either to arbitration or to an enquiry by the Council (Articles 12, 13, and 15). The Covenant also instructed the Council to draw up plans for a permanent Court of International Justice (Article 14), and this was done. This Court was to be competent to hear any legal dispute submitted to it and was also empowered to give advisory opinions on questions referred to it by the Council or by the Assembly.

If arbitration failed, disputes must be submitted to the Council. And if the Council failed to effect a settlement, it could publish a report giving the *facts* and its recommendations for settling the dispute. But on no account could any Member of the League go to war with another under the Covenant *until three months after* the decision on the dispute had been given either by arbitration or by the Council.

Article 16 spoke of the sanctions to be imposed, as described in Chapter 7.

Finally, Article 17: if a dispute arose between a Member-State and a non-Member, or between non-Members, the non-Members were to be invited to become Members for the purpose of the dispute. To sum up: no State, whether a Member of the League or not, could henceforward disturb the world's peace until peaceful methods had been tried.

Special aims

Not least, the League set up commissions and committees to cope with a widening range of world social and technical problems as they arose. Six 'Special Aims' were listed under Article 23 as follows:—

(1) To secure humane labour conditions throughout the world.

(2) To secure just treatment for natives in colonial areas.

(3) To put down traffic in white slaves, opium, and dangerous drugs.

(4) To control traffic in arms and ammunition in less civilised countries.

(5) To secure for all freedom of communications and fair commercial treatment.

(6) To prevent and control disease.

As a prominent staff member pointed out: 'The great political issues discussed at Geneva found a world-wide echo in the press, the radio, and in parliamentary debates. Questions of regional interest were followed with passionate interest in one part of the world and might not even be recorded in other parts. Technical activities in the economic field were universally followed, but interest in the social and humanitarian activities ... was practically restricted to Anglo-Saxon countries as far as the daily press was concerned.'[13] Could not a similar comment be written concerning today's U.N. activities in so many non-political fields?

How the League tackled its worldwide responsibilities through its various Commissions and Committees can be summarised in this way:—

The Health Committee carried on campaigns against disease and laid the working basis of today's World Health Organisation.

The Transport Committee helped to improve and coordinate travel across frontiers and seas.

---

[13] E. F. Ranshofen-Wertheimer, *op. cit.*

The Economic Questions Committee investigated global poverty and unemployment, and strove to reduce tariff barriers between nations.

The Minorities Committee watched over the interests of over 30 million people in Europe, shut off from their own countries, mainly as a result of the First World War.

The Mandates Commission looked after the welfare of indigenous peoples in African and Asian territories, which had once belonged to Germany and Turkey.

The Mandates Commission

So much for the bare bones of the document which became the leading instrument of world affairs for the next two decades and which was to become a generation later the model on which the United Nations, in so many ways, based its own existence. How far its principles were observed, how its obligations were ignored, and how its trust was abused will be the theme of the chapters which follow.

What is the Covenant?

*Short summary of the Covenant of the
League of Nations*

The Covenant was an agreement between nearly all the civilized governments of the world for the better ordering of international relations. To this end all its signatories — the Members of the League — agreed to establish permanent institutions to carry out three purposes: the prevention of the outbreak of war, the removal of the causes of war, and the development of international co-operation.

The following is a brief summary of the provisions of the twenty-six Articles of the Covenant:—

Article 1. — Membership of the League is confined to the forty-two self-governing states or dominions mentioned by name in the Covenant together with those afterwards elected by a two-thirds majority of the Assembly.

Members may retire from the League on giving two years' notice.

Article 2. — The League shall act by means of an Assembly, a Council, and a Secretariat.

Article 3. — At the Assembly each Member may have three representatives, but one vote only.

Article 4. — The Council consists of representatives of Great Britain, France, Italy, and Japan, together with representatives of six other states elected by the Assembly every year. Any other state may send a representative whenever discussions take place which affect its interests.

The Council and the Assembly may both deal with any matter within the sphere of action of the League or affecting the peace of the world.

Article 5. — Important decisions of the Council or Assembly require unanimity.

Article 6. — Provides for the formation of a permanent Secretariat.

Article 7. — Geneva is to be the headquarters of the League. All positions in the League and Secretariat are to be equally open to men and women.

Article 8. — Plans are to be drafted by the Council for the general reduction of national armaments, which the Members agree are necessary for the maintainance of peace.

Article 9. — A permanent Advisory Commission on military, naval and air questions is to be appointed.

Article 10. — A mutual undertaking is given to preserve and maintain the territory and independence of all the Members of the League.

Article 11. — A declaration is made that any threat of war whatsoever concerns the whole League. Any such threat or 'any circumstance whatever affecting . . . the good understanding between nations upon which peace depends' may be brought before the Council by *any* Member of the League.

Article 12. — A mutual undertaking is given by all Members to submit their disputes to judicial settlement, arbitration or enquiry by the Council, and in no case to resort to war until three months after the award or report.

Article 13. — Disputes on questions of fact or international law are generally to be submitted to arbitration.

Article 14. — A Permanent Court of International Justice is to be established (carried out in 1921).

Article 15. — The Council is to enquire into all disputes not otherwise settled, and to endeavour to bring the parties to agreement. If it fails it is to make a report on the merits of the case. If this report is unanimous (except for the parties), the Members agree not to go to war against any state which carries out its recommendations.

Article 16. — A mutual undertaking is given by the Members of the League to combine (by diplomatic pressure, blockade, or, if necessary, armed force) to prevent a resort to war in breach of the above agreements of the Covenant.

Article 17. — Contains provisions regarding disputes between

Members and States which are not Members of the League.

Article 18. — No international Treaty is to be binding unless registered with and published by the Secretariat.

Article 19. — The Assembly is given the power to 'advise' the reconsideration of Treaties and conditions which are out of date.

Article 20. — No obligations inconsistent with the Covenant (e.g. offensive military alliances) are to remain binding on the Members of the League.

Article 21. — International obligations for the preservation of peace are to remain valid.

Article 22. — Contains provisions regarding the Mandates System for backward peoples and territories.

Article 23. — The League is given rights of control or supervision over various international social and economic activities.

Article 24. — All international offices are henceforward to be under the League.

Article 25. — The activities of the International Red Cross for peace-time purposes are to be encouraged.

Article 26. — Provisions for the amendment of the Covenant.

CHAPTER 3

The Key Men

"What we need on the secretariat of the League is not a system but men and women."
— *Carl J. Hambro of Norway at the 10th Assembly*

The shock of the First World War in 1914 was the greater because the new century had showed such promising signs of an ever-shrinking and interdependent world. Peoples were obviously getting closer together as transport and communications improved in speed and equipment. The internal combustion engine, Marconi's 'wireless' and the fantastic airplane—first used extensively in that war—made it more and more incredible that nations should *deliberately* prepare to use their wonderful science and technology to slaughter each other. A modern historian thus describes the pre-war scene:

> In 1914, Europe was a single civilized community, more so even than at the height of the Roman Empire. A man could travel across the length and breadth of the Continent without a passport until he reached the frontiers of Russia and the Ottoman empire. He could settle in a foreign country for work or leisure without legal formalities . . . Nearly everywhere men could be sure of reasonably fair treatment in the courts of law . . . and in nearly all countries something was done to temper the extreme rigours of poverty.[1]

---

[1] A. J. P. Taylor: *From Sarajevo to Potsdam* (Harcourt, Brace & World) 1966.

World links multiply

The shrinking of the world had made it increasingly difficult — and ultimately impossible — for the governments of sovereign states, acting independently, to manage world affairs. International organisations were multiplying across the frontiers on transnational lines.

In 1815, at the Congress of Vienna, there had existed no public international organisation. Not a single piece of international machinery was created through which governments could officially work together on a day-to-day basis. Yet no less than thirty-three public international organisations had of necessity come into existence by 1914. During those one hundred years, unofficial world-wide organisations were also springing up and grew constantly.

Of the thirty-three public organisations mentioned, the best known was probably the Universal Postal Union (UPU). How came it to be formed? The answer well illustrates the beginnings of global administration. Expanding economic and commercial relations inevitably meant increase in postal com-

International conferences:
How they have grown during 100 years

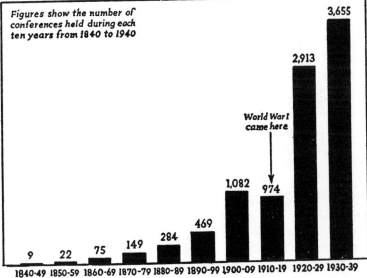

Figures show the number of conferences held during each ten years from 1840 to 1940

World War I came here

3,655

2,913

1,082

974

469

284

149

75

22

9

1840-49 1850-59 1860-69 1870-79 1880-89 1890-99 1900-09 1910-19 1920-29 1930-39

munications. During the first half of the nineteenth century, individual States concluded treaties with each other. However, the first objective of each State was not to facilitate correspondence as such, but to 'make the foreigner pay'. The foreigner did pay; and, as everyone was a foreigner, he frequently paid ridiculously high rates on his foreign postage. Rates were uncertain and extremely variable. There were three different rates between Germany and neighbouring Austria. A business letter mailed from the United States to Australia cost either 5 cents, 33 cents, 45 cents, 60 cents, or 102 cents per half ounce, according to the route by which it was sent. The UPU put an end to anarchy in the mails. Under the 1876 Universal Postal Convention, a Bureau of the UPU, consisting of a Director and eight Assistants, was created in Berne. It has been there ever since, and is nowadays a Specialized Agency of the United Nations.

As steamships multiplied on the trade routes, they brought cholera and plague, as well as goods and passengers. Great Britain and other countries, acting independently, imposed different quarantine restrictions to check the spread of such epidemics. These did not succeed. Isolated action by one government could never be effective in blocking disease. Each epidemic after 1851 was, in fact, followed by an international diplomatic conference to discuss remedies. But for forty years conflicting national interests, as they were called, made concerted action impossible. The logic of facts finally destroyed the fiction of national isolation. When the last epidemic broke out in 1892, it was clear that the interests of *all* nations required common action. The first International Sanitary Convention was signed later in 1892, and was followed by other Conventions. There has been no cholera epidemic in Western Europe since that Convention was signed.

Again, by the Paris Treaty of 1856, a European Commission for Navigation of the Danube was established with a handful of office and engineering staff, who thus had permanent international status. Similarly, the International Institute of Agriculture was set up in 1905 by a Convention between thirty-eight States. The Convention stipulated that the Institute's staff should be international in character. Although they remained mainly Italian, the point was established.

In this way, a novel pattern of international administration emerged, step by step, for the control of health, posts, telegraphs and wireless, and other public services. National interests were slowly being forced to give way to the basic needs of the world as one society. That process could never be reversed. It became clearer as time went on, however, that some central organisation was desirable to bring together and harmonise all these separate bits of international machinery.

The League of Nations Secretariat came not a moment too soon as a necessary co-ordinator. We can never overestimate its significance in the history of peace. The U.N. Secretary-General, the late U Thant, recalled this earlier development in April, 1969, when he unveiled the League's fiftieth anniversary plaque in Geneva. He then said: 'The League has been described as the first organism of international morality — not a coalition against those nations outside the League, but a coalition against the wrong-doing of its own members. This was in itself a tremendous advance in international relationships.' U Thant went on to summarise the League as 'a rallying point, a clearing house which enabled the nations who desired peace to mobilize and concentrate their forces.'

Helping people

Following the International Sanitary Convention of 1892, noted above, the League gradually became the centre of health and welfare projects that overflowed the frontiers. In fact, the League's Health Organisation showed what a great advance had been made on pre-war efforts at international co-operation to keep people well. In 1910, an International Office of Health had been set up in Paris in which thirty-three governments were co-operating. This office was merged with the League Organisation, acting as liaison for fifty-eight co-operating governments.

They had a heavy task from the start. More people had died of epidemic diseases immediately following the war than were killed during the war itself. The League Health Organisation at once grappled with the typhus that had spread from Russia into Poland. Diseases were brought to all parts of the world by troops massed in Europe, especially in Eastern Europe. But Western Europe and the United States itself were spared the worst ravages because of the preventive work organised from Geneva.

Later on, the League regularly published facts and figures on world health conditions. It organised a system of visits by which national health officials could get the best advice and share with each other the latest discoveries. It also sent out health missions to governments in need. Today, its direct successor, the World Health Organisation (W.H.O.) is one of the most active U.N. agencies, which no country can do without.

The League's Health Committee and the International Labour Office co-operated closely in their concern for the health of children. Alongside them, the Committee on Intellectual Co-operation helped the poorest nations to develop their schools and universities. It sent books and materials to students in need and encouraged teachers and students to travel and study in different countries. By publishing text-books about the League, the Committee tried to ensure that in all countries history and geography should be fairly taught to the young.

But perhaps the greatest service to the world's children was the Committee for the Protection of Children and Young Persons set up at Geneva in 1924. The Fifth Assembly adopted the Declaration of Geneva, which was a sort of Childrens' Charter of Human Rights. In this Declaration the nations asserted that:

1. The child must be given the means requisite for its normal development, both materially and spiritually.
2. The Child that is hungry must be fed; the child that is sick must be cured; the child that is backward must be helped; the delinquent child must be reclaimed; and the orphan and the waif must be sheltered and succoured.

3. The child must be put in a position to earn a livelihood and must be protected against every form of exploitation.
4. The child must be the first to receive relief in times of distress.
5. The child must be brought up in the consciousness that its talents should be devoted to the service of its fellowmen.

We might well trace the development of this world declaration on the rights of children into our own times. The work of the United Nations in advancing the welfare of children is one of the best-known of its present-day functions in country after country, not least through the programme of the Children's Fund — UNICEF. It all began at Geneva.

The League also set up an international body to supervise and control the traffic in dangerous drugs. The practice of taking habit-forming drugs was widespread. It was long recognised as a grave menace, to be combated by international action. Smoking a drug made from poppy juice, known as opium, was particularly rampant. In China and Egypt, for example, a large proportion of the population were at some period or another drug addicts. Victims became ruined in

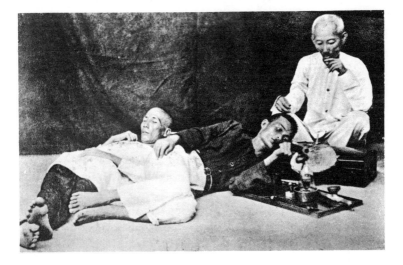

The League began a World Campaign against dangerous drugs — the U.N.
continues it.

health and character, and unable to resist temptation. But it was difficult to prevent smuggling of drugs into China, Egypt, and other countries, for two reasons: the drugs could easily be concealed in unexpected places — table-legs, soles of shoes, tins of jam and false-bottomed boxes; secondly, this traffic was — and still is — very profitable indeed. It became clear, when experts worked on the problem at Geneva, that the smuggling would not be stopped until only those drugs needed for medical and scientific purposes were manufactured in licensed factories.

At last, in 1931, a Convention was adopted to determine the agreed amount to be manufactured, which the different countries declared to be their medical and scientific needs. Yet the difficulties were not yet overcome. Some governments were not strong enough to observe the Convention. In China, a great deal of opium continued to be produced from poppy-fields cultivated by order of rival war-lords. Worse, when Japan left the League, it encouraged the sending into China of opium from Manchuria. However that may be, the League never lost its hold on the drug problem or its faith in its solution. Today, the International Narcotics Control Board at Geneva, which practically all civilised nations support and respect, is recognised to be one of the main checks to this nefarious trade.

A world civil service

Behind all this co-operation was the unobstrusive role of the Secretariat, created under Article 6 of the Covenant as the permanent staff of the League. It was well described as the first international civil service. The invitation of the Swiss authorities to set up the League in Geneva was quickly accepted. The Secretariat was charged first with the collection and distribution of facts and figures from all over the world. That looks an obvious thing to do; but accurate information was to remain the basis of the League's work. The Secretariat became a centre for new international bureaux and commissions as they grew. It became, too, the focus of world diplomacy. As the United States did not belong, Europe was forming its own capital city, for the first time since the days of Rome.

What, then, was this quality that turned the City of Geneva into the Capital of Europe? Geneva has so long stood, like its surrounding Alpine peaks, for so many high achievements of the human spirit that its example has long become the touchstone admired by political historians and social scientists alike. Geneva had already laid a sure foundation for the International Red Cross and given its name to its renowned Geneva Conventions.

Here was a symbol of independence, a centre of reform, and a guarantee of neutrality which all men could respect and acclaim. And these three basic elements also formed the framework of the League's grand design. Without political independence, the League could not develop the unique techniques which gave it its early promise. The reform of human attitudes towards war took the League into many dark corners of that untamed jungle where men are still occupied in destroying men. Neutrality was the very condition of its existence. We do well to ponder the historical and ethical links between the City and the Cause, for a feckless world has yet to acknowledge the debt it owes to Geneva.

"The Reformation Wall" (1909)

The Reformation Wall, built in 1909, is world-famous and in every sense monumental. The four towering figures of Calvin, Farel, de Beze and John Knox remind the dwarf-like humans who gaze up at them today that Calvin's City has always been an international city and the reforms to which it has given birth have been universal in their scope and effect. So when the League of Nations, in the early twenties, held its first annual assemblies in the *Salle de la Réformation,* it continued a prized tradition. Today the mile-long facade of the *Palais des Nations,* which was actually completed in 1938 for the League, has become the European Office of the United Nations, crowded with activity, its corridors and office space expanding with every new task placed upon it. Against the Jura sky-line, with all Geneva at its feet, this beautiful modern *palais* commands a view over blue lake and snow-capped mountains which can hardly be matched in all Europe.

When the League personnel chose Geneva for their home, the oversized Hotel National — renamed *Palais Wilson* after its new incumbent — became its headquarters. Around the *Palais des Nations* itself the permanent organs of the coming World Order now operate as members of the U.N. family.

Geneva Palais des Nations and Mont Blanc.

Nothing that the League achieved has been wasted; it has grown and fructified with the years. Geneva is its birthright.

The Economic and Social Council (ECOSOC) meets each summer in Geneva, bringing hundreds of departmental ministers and their specialist staffs together. The World Health Organisation (WHO), the World Meteorological Organisation (WMO), the International Labour Organisation (ILO), the UN Trade and Development Conference (UNCTAD), the Human Rights Commission, the International Law Commission, and a host of other permanent international bodies, as well as countless voluntary agencies, are nowadays carrying out, as matter of course, the earth's most essential common services. The League's legacy is mankind's richest possession.

The bare recording of their titles, functions and programmes would fill many pages of this book. That is where the League led the way. Yet how much does the average reader of the daily headlines know about the positive works of peace, the constructive tasks of humanity, which proceed, all the year round, from a thousand growing-points of co-operation in this World City?

Although our story revolves around the work of the League, it should be remembered that the very name 'Geneva Con-

International Red Cross Headquarters

vention' has become synonymous with positive and active neutrality. Swiss neutrality has given more to mankind than a legal doctrine. Through two devastating World Wars, hundreds of Red Cross workers, organisers, and Swiss personnel based in Geneva, held unfalteringly in their hands the reins of sanity in a world of warring nations. The International Red Cross motto runs: 'Above all nations is humanity'. That is where the League made its home and tried to practise the Spirit of Geneva.

The neutral man

This idea of a permanent staff following up the decisions arrived at by regular conferences between the Ministers of the Great Powers, was a method that had successfully worked with the various inter-allied bodies during the First World War. These wartime bodies included the Supreme War Council, the Supreme Economic Council, and the Allied Maritime Transport Council. Thus, the war itself had set a working precedent for the League's Secretariat.

'We owe a great debt to the framers of the Covenant,' the former U.N. Secretary-General U Thant once pointed out, 'who, in the space of a few weeks, in an atmosphere of emotion and prejudice engendered by war, succeeded in laying the foundations of an imposing edifice. It represented one of the most positive and constructive acts of the Peace Conference.' As distinct from merely temporary wartime activities, however, the formation of a *permanent* international secretariat was something quite novel in world history. A League senior official has emphasized also its basic difference with earlier diplomatic conferences:

> The world has become one through technological changes; and national independence has given way to national interdependence . . . The international civil service serves the higher interest of international communities in which the national interest of every State has its due share.[2]

---

[2] A. Loveday: *Reflections on International Administration* (Oxford) 1950.

The same authority goes on to underline the psychological significance of the Geneva experiment: 'A real corporate sense did develop in Geneva after the First World War with remarkable rapidity . . . both the League and the ILO were at core European rather than world institutions and the international society reflected the unity of European culture.'

Thus, the League introduced into world affairs a new style of diplomatic neutrality. The League's staff regulations stipulated: 'The officials and Secretariat of the League of Nations are exclusively international officials and their duties are not national but international. By accepting appointment, they pledge themselves to discharge their functions and to regulate their conduct with the interests of the League alone in view. They are subject to the authority of the Secretary-General, and are responsible to him in the exercise of their functions, as provided in these Regulations. They may not seek or receive instructions from any government or other authority external to the secretariat of the League of Nations.' That was quite an innovation in 1920. Not until the Covenant was adopted, were the privileges and immunities of international officials recognised as of worldwide concern.

'Even in cases of serious political conflict,' comments the aforementioned official, 'for example, when the Governments of Fascist Italy and Nazi Germany ceased to be Members and exerted pressure on their nationals to leave the international civil service, several of them, in spite of the 'crisis of loyalty' thus created, resisted the pressure and remained at their posts in the Secretariat.'

This principle of neutrality was observed so strictly, in fact, that the staff regulations required that 'no official of the Secretariat may, during the term of his appointment, accept from any government any honour or decoration except for services rendered before appointment.' The League even discouraged its officials from *wearing* at official receptions decorations which they had received prior to joining. The privilege of being a servant of mankind had to be rigidly preserved, and it was.

What did they do?

Since the external activities of the League will be dealt with in the following chapters, it will suffice at this point to indicate on the diagram below how the main functions of the Secretariat were divided between a dozen or so sections. A few comments follow to amplify the diagram.

The Organisation of the Secretariat

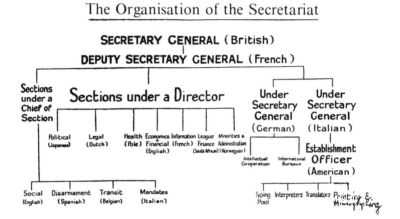

Under the first Secretary-General, Sir Eric Drummond (1919-33), a former high official in the British Foreign Office, whose name was designated in the Peace Treaty itself, the staff numbered about six hundred officials of some fifty nationalities. The Deputy Secretary-General was Monsieur J. E. Avenol, a Frenchman, who later succeeded Sir Eric. The above listing of the nationalities serving as heads of the main departments during the period of Sir Eric's leadership may be taken as a typical cross-section of the successful partnership that prevailed in the Secretariat over nearly two decades.

'Whatever its shortcomings may have been — and they were surprisingly few,' another former League servant has said, 'the League Secretariat will forever serve as a witness to the fact that in spite of the signally unfavourable circumstances prevailing between the time of the signing of the Treaty of Versailles and the outbreak of the Second World War, citizens of more than forty nations, at a time of rampant nationalism, with no precedents to guide them, collaborated as one team for

Sir Eric Drummond, 1st Secretary General (1922)

a common purpose. The experiment of Geneva proved con-
clusively that international administration on a large scale is
possible. This alone should suffice to justify the attempt that
was made.' [3]

Sir Eric Drummond had to build up a secretariat from
scratch. In conformity with the traditions of the British Civil
Service, which were well-known and respected everywhere, it
was assumed that he would follow the adminstrative model of
his country. Even if the methods of recruitment were vague at
first, they were clarified by experience. He aimed primarily to
secure the best available men and women for the jobs to be per-
formed. But in doing so, he had careful regard to selecting his
officials from various nations, including non-Members like the
United States. Thus, the principle of the neutral character of
the Secretariat was maintained from the outset.

The Secretariat became a barometer of world political
weather; the League was the first to be made aware of the shape
of things to come. In the 1930's, however, support of the

---

[3] E. F. Ranshofen-Wertheimer: *The International Secretariat* (Carnegie)
1945.

Secretariat became half-hearted. The natural growth of the early years was arrested. Finance was grudgingly granted, and its international standing was questioned by the German and Italian representatives. The premonition of coming events began to appear and a shadow passed over Geneva.

Unlike the present United Nations, with so high a proportion of its staff working outside its New York headquarters, the structure of the Secretariat remained integrated during the whole of the League's existence. 'Although the Secretariat, with the help of committees of experts, made enquiries regarding forced labour, housing, child welfare, nutrition and refugees, taken as a whole, these external activities of the League were never a major feature of the administration.' [4]

Some of these non-political duties had very broad political implications, however. For example, there was an important article of the Covenant which dealt, indirectly it is true, with secret treaties; it required all League Members to register their treaties with the Secretariat for publication. Article 18 was put into the Covenant to prevent a return to the evil practice of secret undertakings which had done so much to create suspicion and promote military rivalry between countries. No treaty would now bind the peoples whose representatives had signed it until its terms had been publicised to the world by the Treaty Registration Department of the Secretariat. That continues to be the position today under the United Nations.

But as far as the outside world was concerned, the Secretariat itself presented little glamour or romance. 'With the head of the international administration sitting silently throughout the debates, the officials shunning publicity, and no technical breakdown ever occurring, little happened that could make the Secretariat exciting to a public thousands of miles away.' [5] And the same authority goes on to point out: 'The great masses of the world never became actually aware of the existence of this unique experiment in international administration, and the broader lessons it contained for

---

[4] G. Langred: *The International Civil Service* (Sythoff-Oceana) 1963.

[5] E. F. Ranshofen-Wertheimer, *op. cit.*

humanity were practically lost.'

Fortunately, the designers of the U.N. Secretariat after the Second World War have been luckier and wiser men. For them — as we shall note from time to time in the following pages — these broader lessons have been applied to meet humanity's contemporary needs in a way that would have been inconceivable during the short and turbulent course of the League's unique experiment .

Laying foundation stone of Palais des Nations, September, 1929.

PART II

YEARS OF GROWTH

(1921-1929)

CHAPTER 4

The Spirit of Geneva

"There is no doubt that Mankind is once more on the move. The very foundations have been shaken and loosened, and things are again fluid. The tents have been struck, and the great caravan of Humanity is once more on the march."

— *J. C. Smuts,* 1918

Mankind was indeed on the march, but its road was, as we have seen, cluttered with the human and material debris of war. So this Chapter must begin by showing how the League, in its earlier steps, struggled to clear the way in Europe for its main tasks of peace-keeping. It was to economics and finance that the League had to turn first.

The war had brought about a fatal derangement in the action of the gigantic machine that modern industry had become by the early years of the 20th century. Professor Arnold Toynbee pointed out: 'The burning fiery furnace which had been pouring molten wealth for half a century had suddenly become a vortex of destruction, and at the beginning of 1920, when the flames were dying down, it was becoming possible to estimate how much of the wealth and happiness of Western Europe had been consumed.' But the destruction of human values and social stability could not be measured by the casualty returns of the belligerents, he said: 'In addition to the killed, wounded, and shell-shocked combatants, there were the victims of blockade and famine who had perished and the far greater numbers who had been enfeebled permanently in various degrees, and the victims of unemployment arising from the interruption of emigration and international trade.'[1]

The physical destruction which was so visible across the war zones of Belgium, Northern France and Poland, was increased by the deterioration of over-driven plant and over-cultivated land; by the forcible transfer of cattle, rolling-stock, shipping, machinery and valuable property from one community to another. Worse, the depreciation of European currencies in comparison with the American dollar blocked a return to normal commercial relations. Perhaps more serious than all this erosion of life and property was the human despair, the psychological devastation which it left behind. Within this dire context the newly-born League got immediately to work on a variety of complex rescue operations. The extraordinary thing was that hardly a word giving authority for these urgent duties could be found in the Covenant. But it was a good place to begin, all the same — with human beings.

Rescue operations

Conspicuous among these was the financial reconstruction of Austria. In 1922, the little new Austria was on the verge of bankruptcy and the population of Vienna seemed doomed to starvation. An empire of 50 million people had been cut down to 6 million, a third of whom actually lived in Vienna — a head with practically no body to feed and support it. Tens of thousands of dismissed officials from the dismembered cities flocked to the capital for jobs. The distraught Government wildly printed paper notes to pay its swollen army of officials. The Austrian crown catapulted from 24 to the pound sterling to 330,000. There were colossal reparations to pay for having lost the war. In September, 1922, when the Supreme Council of the Allies had abjectly failed to save Austria from collapse, the League appointed a Committee under Lord Balfour's chairmanship to draw up the main guide-lines to put Austria on its feet. On October 4, the League's scheme was accepted by the Governments called in to help. The Austrian Chancellor

---

[1] A. J. Toynbee: *The World After the Peace Conference* (O.U.P.) 1926).

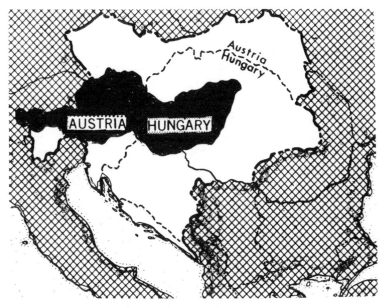

Austria-Hungary before (white) and after (black) the Treaty.

exclaimed: 'Thank God we can say today that the League of Nations has not failed us!'

The scheme called for a series of international loans, guaranteed by League members and under a Commissioner appointed by the League. After a year's concerted effort the result was astonishing. They had managed to balance the national budget, to stabilise the inflated currency, to increase eight-fold savings in the Austrian Banks, to lower the cost of living, and to reduce unemployment within manageable limits. This was a remarkable pioneer programme, with the League acting as focus of effort and co-ordinator for the creditors.

'Austria seemed in 1922,' said Lord Balfour, summing up in February, 1924, his committee's work, 'to have sunk so hopelessly into a morass from which no human resolution, no human ingenuity, no human good fortune would avail to extract her . . . The stabilisation of the currency brought with it that confidence which has enabled the capitalist who had spent his money abroad, to bring it back; it has enabled the home producer to give of his best, knowing that he will reap the fruit of his exertions; and the whole psychology of the community has been changed.'

In this way, the League took the first big step towards the economic recovery of Central Europe: the revival of European markets and the solution of many tangled problems of trade and unemployment which bedevilled most of the unhappy Continent.

The League next turned to do for Hungary and Greece what it had done for Austria. The tangled story of the German reparations problem came to be written later, but it was clear that the Dawes Committee's plan in 1924 — named after its American chairman General Dawes — had at last opened a way for a return of real peace to Europe. This wider financial settlement was based largely on the League's successful earlier experiences with Austria, Hungary and Greece. The League had proved itself to be a working concern.

Reconstruction by stages

Alongside this rebuilding of the bankrupt economies of Europe, the League's early action on behalf of the displaced peoples took two forms:

(1)   Salvage of refugees and prisoners-of-war,
(2)   Protection of minorities.

The brave attempt to deal with the former problem was launched by the First Assembly in 1920. It owed everything to a remarkable personality, who stepped forward at the right moment. Reports showed that nearly half a million prisoners-of-war located in Russia and coming from nations in the east of Europe, had never got home after the war. There were also thousands of Russians still stranded in Germany. Many prisoners starved in dreadfully neglected camps scattered over Siberia. They could not move across Russia, because of the Revolution; they could not get back home at all without outside help. They were desperately short of food and clothes; many were ill, without medicines or attention.

Opposite page: *"It was Nansen who came forward"*

It was Dr. Fridtjof Nansen, the Artic explorer, who came forward at that First Assembly and worked for the League till his death in 1930. The story is as graphic as it is at times incredible. Somehow, he managed to get abandoned trains fuelled and running across and from Russia, and he bought or hired derelict ships; yet he brought home the missing men — some across the Baltic, some across the Black Sea, some right round by sea from Vladivostok. He reported to the Third Assembly in 1922 that the task was finished; all the prisoners that he could find had been restored to their homes. The total cost of the whole operation was less than two million dollars.

The Assembly immediately commissioned him for another crusade. Many white Russians, who did not like the new Bolshevik Government, had fled from Russia into neighbouring countries, particularly to Constantinople and to the Balkans, after the interventionist armies were defeated in North Russia in 1922. Without work or money they were

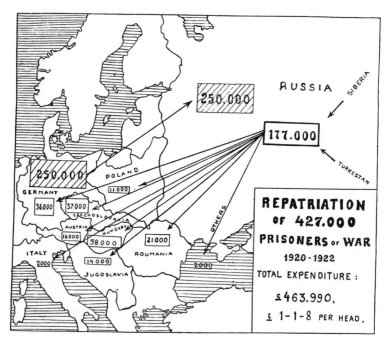

"The task was finished."

helped at first by Red Cross and a few other humanitarian groups, which soon found far more displaced persons than they could cope with. Nansen's first aim was to find countries where their professions and trades were needed, and to persuade the governments to accept them. Many he got into France, where there was no serious unemployment at the time. Some were assisted to migrate to America. Some were found useful jobs in countries nearer Russia; others changed their minds and were willing to go back to Russia. But as the Governments insisted on passports for crossing a border, Nansen had special identity certificates printed for these people without a country. The famous Nansen Passports are still in use today. Fortunately, the International Labour Organisation

A "Nansen" passport.

had by now been set up in Geneva. So when it was a question of trying to place refugees in employment, the I.L.O. took over the task.

Dr. Nansen's energies were next turned to another large group of homeless people. In 1922, the Greeks and the Turks were fighting again in Asia Minor, where many Greeks had lived for generations. The Turks drove the Greeks back to the sea; thousands of men, women and children fled until they reached Smyrna on the coast. There on the seashore, starving and defenceless, they waited for rescue. At once Nansen gathered supplies of flour to feed them, until the refugees could be put on ships for Constantinople and Greece.

But when they poured into Greece in thousands, infectious epidemics came with them. Now the newly-formed Health Section of the League went into action to back up Nansen, just as the I.L.O. had done. The immigrants were collected into temporary camps; though this obviously could not last. Greece was able, however, to raise loans of about forty million dollars from other League members and the United States to help settle her refugees in new villages, to build houses and workshops, and to set them up in farming, fishing, and handicrafts. Prosperous little villages soon grew up where formerly there were no people at all. With the immigrants on their feet as independent workers, Greece herself gained in prosperity. These successes were made possible largely because the League's secretariat was working in the background all the time as an international body that could act speedily in great disasters, without regard to politics, race or nationality.

Thus, the first comprehensive refugee scheme was planned under Nansen's direction and became part of the League's normal programme — though there was not a word about it in the Covenant. The League found, however, that the need to succour the refugees was never at an end. Long after the war, there remained homeless and destitute people spread across Europe and beyond. By 1935, twenty-one years after the first refugees had been driven from their homes, the Nansen Refugee Office at Geneva — which had been set up after Nansen's death to continue his work — had at least a million persons on its books and knew that there existed many thousands more not registered. The Nansen Office continued to find employment for those able to work and to induce Governments to ease the lot of the aged and sick, and the children. These included Russians, Armenians, Assyrians, Turks, and, at that late date 3,300 more who had fled from the Saar when it was returned to Nazi Germany.

The work of helping refugees and displaced persons went on, until war again engulfed Europe. In 1938, the Nansen Office was still functioning at full speed. This was all the more necessary because Jewish and other victims of Nazi rule were then pouring out of Germany. About 100,000 of them needed help desperately; their numbers were growing larger as the Second World War approached. But that sad story of man's inhumanity to man takes us beyond the confines of this book. (The Nansen Medal is still the highest award conferred for distinguished services by the U.N. High Commission for Refugees). The Spirit of Geneva had not failed humanity; though too little of it had existed in the capitals of the world.

Defending minority rights

The statesmen at the Peace Conference realized the seriousness of European minority problems left in the wake of war. They hoped to let each distinct national group that was large enough decide its own political fate. But what was large enough? *Eleven new states* were created out of territories formerly belonging to Germany, Austria-Hungary, and Russia, which had all included millions of minority peoples within their frontiers. But in solving these basic minority problems, new ones were created. Rearrangement of political frontiers created new minorities throughout Central Europe. Their grievances were the more acute since a race which had been dominant and acted with severity towards the minority within its borders, were transformed under the Peace Treaties into subjects of the very race over which it had tyrannized. Bottom dogs now became top dogs.

It was impossible to carve up Europe into as many small

states as there were self-conscious nationality groups. The result was that about 30 million people were still left, from their point of view, on the wrong side of the new frontiers. On the one hand, disappointed minorities became more restive than ever. On the other hand, the newly dominant political groups began to discriminate against their minorities, especially if they were Jews.

What was to be done to protect the oppressed? This was the question with which the League struggled from the start. Some composite states, like Czechoslovakia and Yugoslavia, tried to build themselves upon several-nationality groups. But although Czechs and Slovaks co-operated fairly well, 23 per cent of the population of Czechoslovakia were Germans, the Sudetens, who were certainly not content with their new status as a minority. (This was before the days of Hitler, of course.) While, in Yugoslavia, political life became an internal struggle to balance Serbs and Croats and Slovenes. All this was storing up trouble for the future. What could the League do?

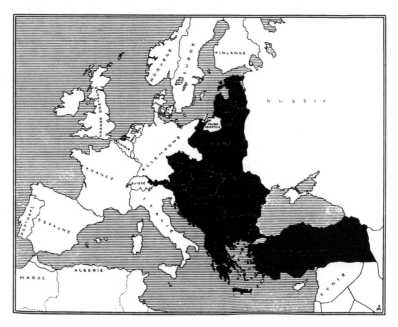

States subject to the Minority rights system under the League.

One solution was to transfer populations from one country to another. In some cases groups of another culture were forcibly uprooted from their homes and moved elsewhere. Greece and Turkey, for example, did eventually exchange populations peacefully on a large scale; Germany and Poland, and Hungary and her new neighbours did so on a smaller scale. But, even with the rare exercise of tolerance and compromise, millions of minorities still remained behind, different in language, race, or religion from their new masters. Facing this unpleasant reality, the Paris Peace Conference had bound certain States to protect their Minorities. This was done by means of Minority Treaties between the Allied and Associated Powers and various European States. But the responsibility for the protection of the Minorities was laid on the League by these same treaties. Again, not a word regarding Minorities had been put into the Covenant, nor was the League ever consulted before this impossible task was assigned to it.

The human rights set out in the Minority Treaties were declared to be matters of international concern. They included protection of life and liberty, free exercise of religion, free use of the mother tongue and local education where there existed a reasonable number of people. Violations were to be reported to the Council of the League, through the Secretariat. This was significant because, formerly, interference by an *outside* power in the interests of a minority would have been regarded as a distinctly unfriendly act. Now it was the unquestionable right of members of the League to intervene when circumstances required it.

How did this protection work out in practice? Alas! it gave rise to much criticism; reforms in procedure were constantly being urged upon the Council. The League's organisation for all this was quite primitive. It consisted of a special section of the Secretariat, together with a three-member sub-committee of the Council. When complaints were received they were first examined by the Secretariat, but had to be communicated at once to the State of which the Minority formed part. Some grievances could be put right at once. Abuses were frequently due to the arbitrary act of some local official. The central government would then often be ready to intervene for the minority on tactful representations from Geneva. But more serious grievances, especially with political overtones, yielded to mediation less readily. The League could rarely go beyond publicising these grievances through its Council discussions. This may not seem to be much; yet still today, under the U.N.'s more sophisticated system and its representative Human Rights Commission, minority rights are a difficult business and their legal and moral protection calls for great patience and diplomatic ingenuity.

The Saar and Danzig

Now we turn to yet another problem child which was, without any mention of parental responsibility in the Covenant, placed by the victorious powers on the League's doorstep. Yet the League handled it with commendable success in the two stages of its operation which fell to it.

The Saar coalfield is neither large nor economically important, but it lies on the boundary of France and Germany. The territory had been occupied by the French during the Napoleonic Wars and was again claimed by them at the end of the First World War as compensation for the destruction by the enemy of coal mines in Northern France. Yet its population of nearly one million had always been entirely German. This was a tough problem for the Peace Conference. In the end a judgment of Solomon was reached. France obtained a fifteen-year lease on the coalfield, while the government of the Saarland was placed indirectly under the League of Nations. The Council appointed Commissioners year by year to cope with problems, but the League had no direct control over Saarland. The Commission itself became a sort of instrument of government — quite an innovation in world affairs — with the French in charge of the territory's economic life.

According to the Paris Treaty, Saar inhabitants were to decide by a free vote in 1935 between three courses: reunion with Germany, transference to France, or continuance of the League regime. But these prospects did not help the League, which had become Saarland's unwilling godmother. As transfer to France was unthinkable, it became necessary for every patriotic German to do everything he could to discredit the Governing Commission in the eyes of the inhabitants. Yet the League had to govern the Saar as a completely impartial agent, holding an even balance between France and Germany.

In 1935, the plebiscite took place and the territory and mines reverted to Germany. What was significant about this plebiscite was the manner in which the League, for the first time in man's history, policed an emotionally charged area with an international police force. The Council made elaborate preparations for the voting in the midst of great anxiety concerning the policy of the Nazi Party in Germany.

Arrangements proceeded smoothly despite heavy campaign activity in the Saar by the Deutsche Front. The main cost of the plebiscite was borne by France and Germany and the

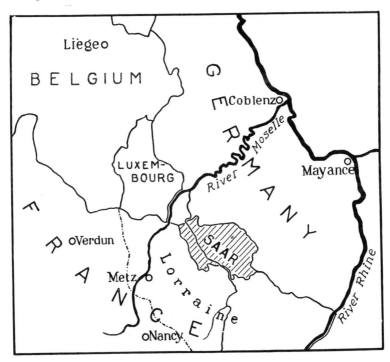

Map of the Saar Territory

Council received pledges from both France and Germany 'to abstain from pressure of any kind' during the campaign. Organisations of foreign officials for the 83 voting areas were created. A plebiscite tribunal was also set up in each of the eight local government districts to hear cases in connection with the voting lists. More important, a special gendarmerie was established to protect the voters and was supplemented by an international armed force of 3,300 men, commanded by a British general under the authority of the Governing Commission. Contingents were drawn from Britain, Italy, Netherlands, and Sweden — clearly an early precedent for the U.N. Emergency Force (UNEF) in the Middle East 20 years later!

The voting went off without any hitch on Sunday, January 13. The vote was so overwhelmingly in favour of Germany that the decision by the Council concerning the legal transfer of sovereignty was much simplified and neither France nor Germany raised controversial questions. The League's servants had again shown their brilliance and competence in organising peaceful change by democratic processes applied to world affairs. (Incidentally, the Saarland fell within the French zone of occupation after 1945 and France again tried to detach the area; but by the agreement reached with West Germany in 1956, the territory was restored to Germany and it became the tenth Land in the present Federal Republic.)

The status of Danzig differed materially from that of the Saar. The area was roughly the same and the population was about half a million; but, while the Saar was controlled by a League Commission, the Treaty pronounced Danzig a Free City with its own Senate and Chamber. In addition, á League High Commissioner was appointed to hold the balance between the City and its neighbour Poland — another near impossible task.

What was Danzig? Until the war, Danzig was one of the great ports of Germany at the mouth of the broad Vistula. All the trade of the Polish hinterland passed down to the port. When the three sections of pre-war Poland — Russian, Austrian, and German — were united under the Peace Treaty, the new State was given access to the sea by a corridor running

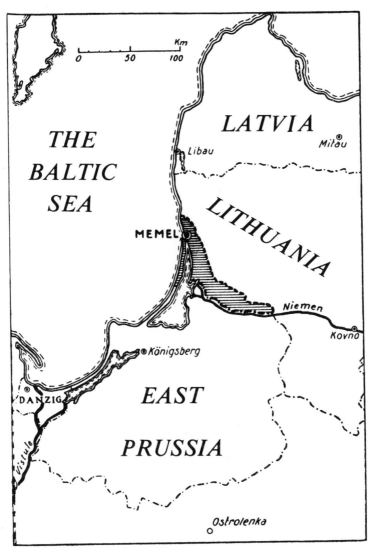

Danzig and Memel

down the Vistula valley. But the Poles were bitterly disappointed that the Peace Conference decided not to give Danzig to Poland. How could they? On the one hand, Danzig was German through and through; to transfer it forcibly to Polish sovereignty would create a powerful and turbulent minority, and it certainly would be against the Wilsonian principles of self-determination. On the other hand, the claims of Poland to the normal use of the port were unquestioned. So the ingenious expedient was devised of severing the city from Germany without uniting it with Poland. Another judgment of Solomon!

Poland was therefore given legal rights in such matters as railways, customs, and the free use of the port. One role of the High Commissioner was to give an impartial ruling in the name of the League on any matter in dispute between Poland and the Free City. From such rulings an appeal lay to the League Council. Gradually, however, the habit of settlement grew by direct negotiation, through the mediation of the High Commissioner or officials of the Secretariat at Geneva. The Danzig currency was put on a sound basis in accordance with a plan prepared by the League's Financial and Economic Organisation. A good point about Danzig's constitution was that no-one was to use the territory as a naval or military base. The Danzig scheme, like the Saar regime, proved to be a vitalizing experiment from which lessons could be derived that might be applicable elsewhere in Europe — had the League been given the time.

The sacred trust

Again, the League broke new ground with its Mandates device. This innovation opened a new perspective on Woodrow Wilson's plea for national independence. As the League developed, it transformed the existing colonial system on which the dominance of the Great Powers had rested for centuries. Only today can one appreciate the sweeping changes the Mandates system introduced. The present United Nations is tackling the last remnants of the colonial era; the few remains of the Trusteeship territories in the Pacific have almost disappeared. But this process of de-colonisation, as it is now called, goes back directly to the sacred trust imposed on the whole League membership by the Mandates scheme.

The full story of how the advanced nations had handled the

'backward peoples' in their colonies had rarely made pleasant reading. There had been growing criticism among private citizens and publicists in the Western World concerning colonial mismanagement and exploitation. Scathing indictments like E. D. Morel's *Red Rubber,* exposing the Belgian atrocities and inhumanities in the Congo, were being widely discussed before the First World War. The exploitation of the weaker races of Africa and Asia for the benefit of a single powerful European state had its dangers for other states too. Traders and manufacturers of non-colonial countries naturally desired a share in the raw materials and other wealth which such 'backward' areas produced. So it was also to lessen the international rivalry and jealousy to which the old colonialism had given rise that the victors themselves acclaimed the new system of the Mandates. Wilson found considerable support, therefore, for his plea not to turn over the ex-enemy's possessions this time as mere spoils of war. General Smuts was one of the main architects of the new system, supported by Lord Robert Cecil of England.

Hence, the Allied Powers at the Paris Peace Conference in 1919 divided up the German African colonies between different Mandatories, and they similarly distributed Turkey's lost possessions in Asia. Only the Allied Powers were chosen to be Mandatories. The League's task consisted first in approving the terms of the Mandate drawn up with each mandatory power, under which the trust was to be exercised; and, second, in exercising, through its Permanent Mandates Commission, the ultimate responsibility for the good administration of each mandated territory.

More important, perhaps, was the double protection offered to the colonial peoples themselves. First, the advanced nations had to act as trustees on behalf of the League of Nations as a whole, and to govern these territories on the conditions which the Council laid down. The most vital principle in each case was that "the well-being and development of such peoples form a sacred trust of civilisation." In pursuance of this trust, the trustees undertook to prohibit such abuses as the arms traffic, which often had encouraged disastrous tribal wars; slavery and the slave trade, and forced labour contracts (which were little better than slavery); and the liquor traffic. They were forbidden to militarize the native subjects by building up greater forces than would be needed to defend the territories themselves; and they had to safeguard the inhabitants from external pressure, not only in economic problems, but with regard to all the social problems resulting from the contact between the 'civilized' and the 'primitive' peoples of the world.

A second safeguard lay in the proven efficiency and broad sympathies of the Mandates Commission itself, as well as in the opportunities provided for a public airing of abuses from the Assembly platform. The success of the Commission was largely due to the fact that it was composed of distinguished private citizens, and not representatives of Governments as such. Its main business was to examine reports sent in by Mandatory States on how they had administered their trusts.

Before we look at the functioning of a sample Mandate, however, we should recall that the Mandates were divided into these three categories (the name of the Mandatory appearing in brackets):

'A.'   Palestine (Great Britain), Syria and Lebanon (France);
'B.'   Tanganyika (Great Britain), Togoland and Cameroons (Great Britain and France), Ruanda and Urundi (Belgium);
'C.'   South-West Africa (Union of South Africa), the North Pacific Islands (Japan), Samoa (New Zealand), German New Guinea and Nauru (Australia).

For our sample Mandate let us briefly examine the case of Great Britain in respect of that area formerly part of German East Africa, which became Tanganyika. The mandate for Tanganyika required the British Government to 'promote to the utmost the material and moral well-being and the social progress of its inhabitants.' In particular, the mandatory power undertook to abolish slavery and suppress the slave trade; to prohibit forced labour; to exercise strict control over the arms and liquor traffic; to safeguard natives' rights in land transfer;

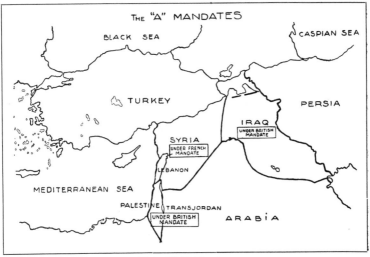

Map of "A" Mandates.

to ensure freedom of conscience and worship; and to keep an open door economically for all League members to share and share alike in trade facilities. No military or naval bases could be established in the territory nor could any native military force be organized for outside use. Similar provisions applied in all other Class 'B' mandates.

One example of how the Permanent Mandates Commission assisted the people of Tanganyika and its neighbour, Ruanda and Urundi, occurred in 1923. The frontier between the two territories (respectively in trust to Britain and Belgium) ran right through the land of certain native tribes. The homes of the tribes were consequently divided from the places where they grazed their flocks and herds. This political division of their land broke up their tribal system — so the Commission found — and caused them loss and hardship. It suggested, therefore, that they should devise a new frontier which would unite these tribal lands. Britain and Belgium made the new treaty that was needed and secured its confirmation by the League. They retraced their frontier, and Britain handed over to the Belgians a great tract of fertile land. Note that this action was taken solely in the interests of the people — something new in colonial history.

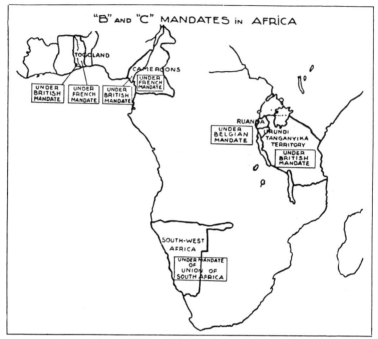

Map of "B" and "C" Mandates in Africa.

The 'A' and 'C' classes were on a somewhat different footing. The former concerned nations approaching the stage of independence. The mandatory's function consisted mainly in giving what is termed 'administrative advice and assistance', and we need not carry the description further.

But the latter category comprised territories which it had been decided were best administered as an integral part of the Mandatory's own possessions. Nonetheless, it was still strictly laid down that 'the Mandatory shall promote to the utmost the material and moral well-being and the social progress of the inhabitants.' And the same prohibitions regarding the slave trade and forced labour applied as in the 'B' Mandates. In the case of the liquor traffic, for example, the 'C' Mandates was even more rigorous and the supply of alcohol to 'natives' was prohibited altogether. Military and naval bases and military service were equally prohibited in the 'C' Mandates.

The unhappy fact is that, although all the Mandates which

still remained after World War II became Trust Territories under the United Nations, the single remaining Mandate today, South West Africa, was a 'C' territory which the Government of South Africa has consistently refused to bring within the United Nations system, though resolutely pressed to do so. In consequence, this oppressed and tormented nation — now called Namibia — has been declared by both the World Court and the U.N. Geneva Assembly to be a legal trust of the United Nations itself. Steps have been taken eventually to break South Africa's stronghold, and a U.N. Commissioner and Council have been appointed for Namibia. Once again, an understanding of the League's operations is essential to appraise today's happenings.

A footnote might be added on what the League did towards abolishing slavery, which had so long been an international problem. By Article 23 of the Covenant, Member States promised to secure just treatment of the native inhabitants of terri-

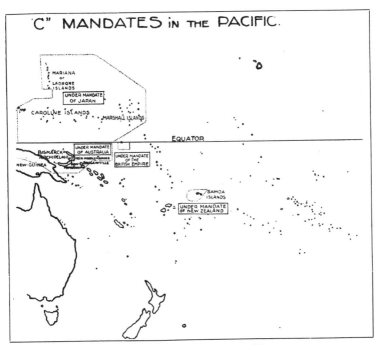

Map of "C" Mandates in the Pacific.

tories under their control. Mandatories were pledged, as we saw in Article 22, to prohibit the slave trade. The League set up several detailed inquiries into slavery and a disturbing report was made to the Assembly in 1925. This was followed by an International Slavery Convention in 1926. Progress was little but steady. By October, 1930, out of 47 States who had signed the Convention, 33 had ratified it. But Ethiopia, France, and China had not then ratified, while Japan, Mexico, and the Soviet Union had not signed at all. Slowly, world opinion was being focussed on this abomination. Under the U.N. more serious action has been followed in the name of Human Rights; but again it was the League that prepared the way.

Can justice be done?

To the right and left of the diagrams on page 54 we note that the main organs of the League were flanked by a world court and a world labour organisation. To these two important bodies we must devote a few pages. Both of them still operate today, intrinsically on the same basis as when they were planned in the early twenties. Both deal with the concept of justice — justice between nations and justice between men. The one is an instrument of international law, the other an instrument of social law. Both were created to promote world peace.

The Permanent Court of International Justice, as it was called, looked back to the efforts which were made before the war (described in Chapter 2) to replace war by arbitration in world relations. It is not surprising that the Court established its seat at The Hague, in a building called The Peace Palace. The Covenant provided (Article 14) that plans for such a Court should be drawn up by the League Council. The project was put in hand at once, approved by the Assembly in 1920; the first judges were elected during the Assembly of 1921; and the Court came into existence in January, 1922.

Previous attempts to set up a world court had broken down through failure to agree on a method for appointing judges. The existence of the League, with its stress on the settlement of

disputes without war, now provided a practical method. It consisted of two parallel elections by the League Council and by the Assembly. Only those candidates chosen by both bodies were declared elected; the voting continued till Council and Assembly were both agreed on all the judges. This method is still in use today under the U.N.

The Court consisted of eleven judges and four deputy judges (today it is 15 full judges) elected on the basis of the same qualifications required in their own countries for the highest judicial offices. The main forms of civilization and the principal legal systems of the world had to be represented on the Bench. Not more than one candidate of the same nationality could be elected. The judges were (and still are) elected for terms of nine years and are eligible for re-election. No judge could exercise any political function or do other professional work. In order to protect them against political pressure, it was provided that no judge could be dismissed unless he failed in his duty. A Registrar of the Court handled the clerical work.

Although the Statutes of the Court were amended somewhat in 1946, when the U.N. took over the work and assets of
the League, and the title was changed to International Court of
Justice, the general functions of the Court have remained
practically unchanged for nearly half-a-century. Between 1922
and 1939 (the period covered by this book) it dealt with no less
than 79 cases, of which 51 were 'contentious' — which means
that states had referred these disputes to the Court for legal
settlement. 28 other cases were 'advisory opinions', given by
the Court for the guidance of the League when the Council
asked for it. Many knotty problems before the Council were
cleared up in this way by the Court. From the start, an
American judge has been a member of the Bench; special rules
allowed non-members of the League (and later the U.N.) to
have their nationals elected.

Only governments could appear as parties before the Court.
If an individual has a grievance against another government,
he must get his own government to present his case. This
happened in 1924 in the case of a Greek subject who had claims
against the British Government under the Palestine mandate;
the Greek Government appeared before the Court on his
behalf. Again, only those cases go to the Court which both
parties *agree* to submit to it. This means that one party cannot
force its opponent to appear. When, however, a country put
into a treaty a clause providing *that any* dispute should be
settled by the Permanent Court, then that party was bound to .
go before the Court.

A special clause in the Court's statutes, which has been much
discussed over the years, is called the 'optional clause'. By
signing this clause, many States have agreed in advance that
they will take to the Court any legal dispute arising between
them. At the 11th Assembly, Britain announced that Britain
and all the Dominions would accept this compulsory
jurisdiction. Their example was followed by many other states:
soon all the Great Powers of Europe and over half the membership of the League of Nations agreed to accept the compulsory
jurisdiction of the Court. Incidentally, the United States was

not one of these; but this event constituted an advance in world confidence in international justice all the same.

In the Wimbledon Case in 1923, the issue arose as to whether, as the Kiel Canal had been declared by the Versailles Treaty open to the ships of all nations, Germany was justified on grounds of neutrality in refusing passage to a vessel laden with arms for Poland, then at war with Russia. A German judge took his seat on the Bench temporarily, since a party to a dispute is entitled to have one of its nationals on the bench for that particular case. The verdict went against Germany by nine votes to three.

Great Britain appeared before the Court in 1925, as the mandatory power for Iraq, to support the League Council's competence to fix the frontier between Turkey and Iraq. The Court handed down an advisory opinion directing the League Council how to handle the dispute. In two other advisory opinions the Court found in favour of Germany against Poland. And so on — more and more nations began to use the Court to settle questions they could not settle by themselves.

In spite of the rudimentary state of international law at that time and the attitude of some nations towards the Court, its successes greatly surpassed all expectations. "The Permanent Court has, since it opened its doors in 1922, rendered more than sixty Judgments and Advisory Opinions, and in no instance has any party to the litigation defied the authority of the Court by refusing to give effect to its decision . . . the output of international law from judicial and arbitral sources since the First World War has been prodigious."[2]

Labour is not a commodity

When the 1919 Peace Conference adopted Part XIII of the Treaty, the International Labour Organisation was created. That part of the Treaty remains to this day the foundation stone of the I.L.O. It was the work of fifteen men who formed the Commission on International Labour Legislation. They went to Paris convinced that world peace depended as much

---

[2] Lord Arnold McNair, former President of the Court.

PARTIE XIII.

TRAVAIL.

___

SECTION I.
ORGANISATION DU TRAVAIL.

___

Attendu que la Société des Nations a pour but d'établir la paix universelle, et qu'une telle paix ne peut être fondée que sur la base de la justice sociale;

Attendu qu'il existe des conditions de travail impliquant pour un grand nombre de personnes l'injustice, la misère et les privations, ce qui engendre un tel mécontentement que la paix et l'harmonie universelles sont mises en danger, et attendu qu'il est urgent d'améliorer ces conditions: par exemple, en ce qui concerne la réglementation des heures de travail, la fixation d'une durée maxima de la journée et de la semaine de travail, le recrutement de la main-d'œuvre, la lutte contre le chômage, la garantie d'un salaire assurant des conditions d'existence convenables, la protection des travailleurs contre les maladies générales ou professionnelles et les accidents résultant du travail, la protection des enfants, des adolescents et des femmes, les pensions de vieillesse et d'invalidité, la défense des intérêts des travailleurs occupés à l'étranger, l'affirmation du principe de la liberté syndicale, l'organisation de l'enseignement professionnel et technique et autres mesures analogues;

Attendu que la non-adoption par une nation quelconque d'un régime de travail réellement humain fait obstacle aux efforts des autres nations désireuses d'améliorer le sort des travailleurs dans leurs propres pays;

Les Hautes Parties Contractantes, mues par des sentiments de justice et d'humanité aussi bien que par le désir d'assurer une paix mondiale durable; ont convenu ce qui suit:

CHAPITRE PREMIER.

ORGANISATION.

___

Article 387.

Il est fondé une organisation permanente chargée de travailler à la réalisation du programme exposé dans le préambule.

Les Membres originaires de la Société des Nations seront Membres originaires de

Part XIII was one part of the Peace Treaty that has stood the test of time and is still the foundation of the I.L.O.

6 Genève - Bureau International du Travail

Geneva - Bureau International du Travail

upon social as upon political justice. They saw that universal machinery to solve social problems was as urgent as what the League was going to do to solve political problems.

Why was this so important? A long road had been travelled to Versailles — a cruel road that had led through the antiquated mines, mills and workshops of the Industrial Revolution in which millions of men, women and children toiled under inhuman conditions. Social reformers had long battled to improve the lot of the working masses. Men like Robert Owen of England, an enlightened employer, sought to demonstrate that the welfare of the workers did not detract from the business success of the employer. Quite the contrary. Daniel Legrand, an Alsatian manufacturer of France, had lobbied European governments to put better working conditions into international agreements. Men like Samuel Gompers of the A.F.L. (who was Chairman of the Paris Commission) had given their lives to help raise social conditions in their own countries. These pioneers for the rights of labour had set in motion a chain reaction which led directly to the creation of the I.L.O. in 1919. Now their leadership for labour peace had taken on world proportions.

The dynamic first Director General was Albert Thomas. With him is Edward Phelan of England who became Director General in 1941 until 1948.

The I.L.O. differed from the League in two ways. It operated from a separate office in Geneva, as an autonomous part of the League. Its first Director-General was a dynamic Frenchman, Albert Thomas. But the enduring strength of the I.L.O. rested on its 'tripartite' character. It had a structure uniting governments, employers and workers in common action. It survived the Second World War — being the only major League of Nations 'department' to do so. It then became the first specialised agency of the United Nations, devoted to social and labour questions.[3]

---

[3] A detailed account of the I.L.O. has been written by the present author under the title *Labour Faces the New Age,* published in the "Workers' Education Manuals" by the I.L.O. (Geneva).

"Universal and lasting peace can be established only if it is based upon social justice" — these words, taken from its Constitution, are the mainspring of I.L.O. action. Its three working principles are:

(1) labour is not a commodity;
(2) poverty anywhere is a danger to prosperity everywhere;
(3) all human beings, irrespective of race, creed or sex, have the right to pursue their well-being and spiritual development in conditions of freedom, dignity and economic security.

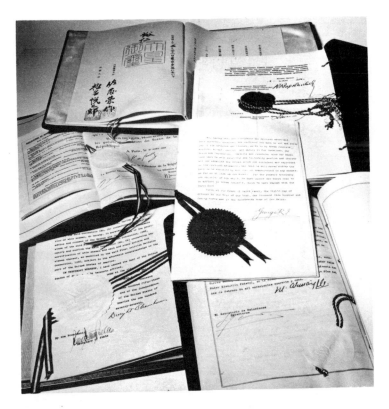

International treaties regulating labour conditions look like this.

For 50 years one of the key jobs of the I.L.O. has remained the same, namely, to set up *standards* in the fields of labour law, social welfare and human rights. In this overall period 260 Labour Conventions and Recommendations have been adopted by the International Labour Conference. They have been one of the main influences for improving social law throughout the world. The I.L.O. founders laid down that the improvement of labour legislation, as it is called, was to be worked out by a Conference composed of government, employers' and workers' representatives, instead of governments alone. Decisions which received two-thirds majority are sent to member-states for putting into national law or for other action. Thus a link was (and still is) established between the Geneva body and the national law-makers.

The diagram below shows how the I.L.O. was constituted both at the time of the League and, with one or two small changes, exists today:

International Labor Organization

Each member state sends four delegates

2 government   1 management   1 worker

TO

INTERNATIONAL LABOR CONFERENCE
which examines social problems and adopts "Conventions" for sending to governments

ELECTS

GOVERNING BODY
Government (16)
Management (8)
Worker (8)

CONTROLS

INTERNATIONAL LABOR OFFICE

CHIEF ACTIVITIES

Research   Investigations   Technical assistance   Publications

International Labour Conventions are conceived as guidelines for national action, but become binding obligations when ratified by member States. Governments are required to report each year to the I.L.O. on the steps they have taken to apply the Conventions they have ratified. The number of ratifications has grown to over 4,000 today.

Many have dealt with the improvement of living and working conditions, such as hours of work, protection of women and young workers, safety and hygiene at work, social security and wages. Others have dealt with factory inspection, employment services, minimum wage fixing, freedom of association, freedom from compulsory labour, and equal treatment in employment. Workers' education and training have always had a high priority in I.L.O. projects.

Naturally, the I.L.O. could not in its early stages do a great deal to change the industrial conditions in countries where higher standards had already been achieved. But it did much to raise working conditions in backward countries, particularly in the Far East. Less advanced countries like India, Japan, China and Persia all responded favourably to the influence of the I.L.O.

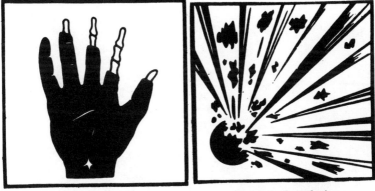

Danger of corrosion
Danger de corrosion
Peligro de corrosión

Danger of explosion
Danger d'explosion
Peligro de explosión

"Safety at Work". Thanks to I.L.O. these danger symbols have been accepted across the world in factories and other work-places.

For example, hours of labour were much shortened in India and the minimum age for the employment of children raised from nine years to twelve. In Japan the employment of children under twelve years of age was prohibited. In China decrees limiting hours and age were promulgated, though the political chaos exisiting in that country made the application of these reforms difficult. In Persia the conditions of child labour in the carpet factories were greatly improved. Little children who spent 12 hours a day in cramped and unhealthy conditions were no longer allowed to suffer in this way.

There is no doubt that the pioneer work of the I.L.O. led to immense worldwide social programmes over the years. These advances are still proceeding today under the various agencies of the U.N. Again, in the area of human relationships, the League of Nations was a foundation well and truly laid.

International Labour Conference held in GENEVA, Switzerland, in October 1923. The first Director Albert THOMAS is seated in right foreground.

CHAPTER 5

Organising Peace

"If the new and frightful weapons of destruction, which are now at the disposal of the nations, seem destined to abridge the duration of future wars, it appears likely, on the other hand, that future battles will only become more and more murderous."
— *Henri Dunant, Founder of the Red Cross (1862)*

Woodrow Wilson had always placed moral force first, 'but if the moral force of the world is to prevail,' he stressed, 'it must have a means by which it can be organised.' This point was taken further by Professor C. K. Webster, a British historian, who said: 'Once it is organised, then the amount of armed force which it will be necessary to place at its disposal will be such that no armed force can challenge the moral force . . . It was impossible for Woodrow Wilson to work out all the machinery necessary in the short time in which the Covenant of the League of Nations was made. Ultimately, of course, the success of any such plan depends on the fact that the organisation should be a world one. Woodrow Wilson could never think except in terms of a world organisation.' [1]

In this chapter, we shall try to come to grips with this intangible relationship of moral and military force, which can be summed up in the word 'security'. Security lay at the heart of the League's dilemma — especially as the League never reached its aim of being a universal organisation. First, we can

---

[1] C. K. Webster: *What the World Owes to President Wilson* (address reprinted in the U.S.A. Congressional Record for January 10, 1930).

consider how the League actually contributed to security by *preventing* war; secondly, how it sought to mobolise security by means of 'mutual assistance'; and, thirdly, how it struggled to bring about all-round disarmament as a *sine qua non* of security.

Preventing war

One prime example may suffice to show how the League's machinery stopped a war. In the autumn of 1922, suddenly and without warning, the army of Yugoslavia crossed the frontier into Albania. They sacked and looted Albanian villages, and marched on the capital, Tirana. All communication with the outside world was cut off. The intentions of the invaders were never disguised: they planned to establish themselves at Durazzo on the Adriatic, and present the world with a *fait accompli*. The Balkans had seen such take-overs before. It would be difficult to exaggerate the consequences that might have followed if the aggressors had succeeded.

The League said: "No!" Under Article XI of the Covenant, the Council had to meet at once to consider any war or threat of war. The Covenant declared it to be the friendly right of any Member of the League to bring any such emergency to the notice of the Assembly or Council. The question of war in the Balkans was raised at once in the British House of Commons and the Prime Minister wired the Secretary-General of the League asking for an immediate meeting of the Council. One result was that a pending Yugoslav loan became unnegotiable on the London market; the Yugoslav exchange rates fell all over Europe. War did not pay! When the League Council met a few days later in Paris the Yugoslav delegates expressed contrition and announced that their troops would withdraw at once north of the frontier. That promise was fulfilled. The Yugoslav army withdraw from Albania within two days and the war came abruptly to an end.

Only a little war — no doubt — but if it had continued for several more weeks Italy would have been drawn in and another conflagration would be in full blaze. This capsule example demonstrates that the League's machinery to stop war could work if one essential condition was fulfilled, namely, the support of public opinion — without which no democratic institution can flourish or even survive.

The power of the Assembly to implement world opinion was once again illustrated by the Corfu incident the following year. The unanimous and immediate condemnation of Mussolini's action in bombarding and seizing that peaceful island was the decisive factor in terminating warlike acts between Italy and Greece. South Eastern Europe was again saved from a general conflagration. The League's handling of this matter was mainly the work of the Council, but the incident reflected the whole-hearted concern of the Assembly as a world-wide sounding-board. 'Had the League not existed, a resort to arms would almost inevitably have taken place,' was the British Prime Minister's verdict.

During the first dozen years of its existence nearly *fifty* political disputes were brought before the League. Some of these came to the League under Peace Treaties, and others were referred to it by the Governments of Member States. Most of them were dealt with by the Council; a few by the Permanent Court, as we noted above. These disputes differed in type and importance. Some involved an actual breach of the peace. In four instances — between Yugoslavia and Albania in 1921, Greece and Bulgaria in 1925, Turkey and Iraq in 1924-6, and Columbia and Peru in 1932 — the League was able to stop a war after fighting had actually begun. These may not have been big wars as such; but it is impossible to say that they could have been localised if the League had not intervened. These were dangerous years, but the League was truly organising peace.

Even where the League was not successful at first, it helped to stop war in the long run. With Bolivia and Paraguay in 1928 pacific settlement was agreed upon in eight days at Geneva. This was called the 'Chaco problem'. But owing to local delays, for which the League was not to blame, fighting broke out again and undid the arrangements for a settlement. Owing to uncertainty as to what the rival claims were, inaccessibility from the sea, and pressure groups outside the League, the conflict dragged on. But the League was able to confine the scope of hostilities; at one point even to instiute the first use of an arms embargo to limit the war. Fighting finally came to an end in 1935 through negotiations with the help of neighbouring States, but by methods persistently urged on them by the League.

Peaceful change

Although the turbulent 1930's will be dealt with in the next chapter, it should be recalled that the League frequently reduced the fear of imminent war by intervening in national disputes. We have already seen this happening in regard to the Saar in 1934; likewise it mediated in a bitter quarrel between Yugoslavia and Hungary in 1935. On both occasions it was the British Government which had taken initiative, pressing for full use of League machinery. The absence of the United States was being increasingly felt at this time. Looking back, it can be seen that without the international police force set up in the Saar, the plebiscite could never have been conducted without bloodshed. And, if the deep antagonisms behind the Yugoslav-Hungarian dispute had not been brought to the surface at Geneva, a violent explosion in central Europe would have been a question only of weeks.

Because the naked aggressions of several Great Powers in the thirties have taken up so much space in contemporary history books, the growing role of the League as a peace-maker has been largely overlooked.

'Wherever the League machinery,' said Lord Robert Cecil at the 13th Assembly, 'has been fairly and genuinely applied, without fear and hesitation, it has produced admirable results.' Many of the disputes which the League had to deal with had aroused wide and bitter discussion. Some had caused tension between other countries as well. The League was not able to settle all these political quarrels finally, but it always helped to reduce the causes of conflict by calming public opinion.

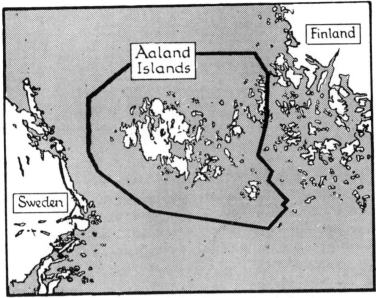

The Aaland Islands

As cases in point, the Aaland Islands conflict in 1920-21, arising from Finland's claim to sovereignty and the Swedish character of the islanders, was settled through the League on the basis of impartial findings from League observers, which were accepted by both Finland and Sweden — again setting a precedent for U.N. mediation today.

Then, in the boundary quarrel centring on the possession of Vilna, a city which had been occupied by Poland since 1920, but claimed by Lithuania, the League prevented the area from becoming a scene of armed conflict. Another legacy of the Versailles Treaty, the Upper-Silesian Settlement of 1921, as it was called, was based on the plebiscite required by the Treaty; but an impartial Commission appointed by the League managed to preserve the economic unity of the territory over a difficult transitional period. Finally, Memel, another danger spot on the frontier of Lithuania, had before the war been part of East Prussia, but was handed over by the Versailles Treaty for disposal.* After endless discussions as to what would happen to this German city, the League Council appointed an

* See map on page 99.

impartial Committee under a neutral chairman, an American. A convention was drawn up by which Memel possessed autonomy within specified limits under Lithuanian general sovereignty. Although friction continued between the German population and the Lithuanian Government over Memel's autonomy for some years, its parliament or Diet, with the Germans having 25 seats and Lithuania 4, was still meeting normally by 1935. Again, a danger spot was contained.

The foregoing are specific examples which, one after another, came before the League Council for settlement or other solution. It seemed a never-ending stream, but it revealed to mankind a new technique for dealing with disputes between nations. No wonder hope and expectation grew in the late twenties for a stronger and better League! It really worked. The League was proving itself every day to be an essential agency of peaceful adjustment and change. This phase of the League's accomplishment is so often forgotten or overlooked; but the founding fathers had built better than they knew.

Search for security

The League had been given the impossible task of implementing the Treaty of 1919 with Germany and the four other treaties which had followed with Germany's allies: Austria, Bulgaria, Hungary and Turkey. France, particularly, was stridently calling for national security. So the League set about this impossible task of finding what came to be termed collective security.

The first such effort came to nothing. It was called the Treaty of Mutual Guarantee of 1923, by which all the States were expected to combine in defence of anyone attacked. It declared aggressive war to be an international crime. But the Treaty depended on a State reducing its armaments first. The guarantee or security element was reaffirmed later in the Locarno Treaty and in the Kellogg Pact, but the 1923 Treaty failed to secure the consent of important Powers and so was dropped.*

* This frantic search for 'security' is examined at greater length in the author's article 'A Search for World Order' in the volume *Foundations of Peace and Freedom* (ed. Ted Dunn) published by Christopher Davies (1975).

Then, they tried again. In 1924, a more universal plan followed, called the Geneva Protocol. It added the principle of Compulsory Arbitration to Security and Disarmament. It was called a 'guarantee' Treaty. It provided an automatic system for the settlement of all disputes. Failure to accept arbitration would be regarded as the test of aggression. The Council was to declare a League blockade against it. This was pretty drastic, but the Protocol was rejected by Great Britain, so could not be put into force, although France and other powers were quite willing, it seemed, to sign it.

Though the Protocol was never adopted in its original form, its influence had a strong effect on the development of arbitration. The words of Robert de Traz, a veteran Swiss observer at Geneva, could hardly be more to the point: 'The Protocol, that great idea of 1924 which evoked so much rejoicing, proved a failure; yet from an agreement which, in its generality, was as yet impossible of realization, emerge, in increasing number, particular agreements.' [2]

The League did some remarkable work in developing the procedure of arbitration. As we noted in Chapter 1, the idea of arbitrating international disputes had been gaining favour before the First World War, as a means of avoiding armed conflicts. The Covenant itself was the biggest arbitration treaty up to that time. Arbitrate, don't fight! More was done during the League period than at any other period of history to improve the machinery of peaceful settlement.

What were the League's rules which were intended as substitutes for war? Articles 12 and 13 laid down the rules for arbitration and judicial settlement; Article 14 provided, as we have seen, for the permanent court; and Article 15 dealt with mediation, conciliation and reports by the Council. Under these rules no signatory of the Covenant had the right to go to war *without first* allowing the Council to examine the problem and, if possible, settlement by a third party. This statesmanlike and commonsense plan could have worked a revolution in international relations — had it been observed.

By 1935, when the war clouds began to gather around the

2 R. de Traz: *The Spirit of Geneva* (Oxford) 1935.

League, there existed 400 new arbitration treaties, and their number was continually growing. 300 of these were treaties for 'pacific settlement of international disputes' erecting new bulwarks against war. One of these was known in 1928 as the General Act for the compulsory settlement of 'every kind' of international quarrel. By the close of 1935 this new Treaty had been ratified by 22 States, including members of the British Empire, France, Italy and Spain. Another Convention to Prevent War called for the cessation of fighting and withdrawal of troops within frontiers. This Convention also was signed by 22 States.

All these desperate efforts to find a way out from war might seem somewhat academic nowadays. They can best be understood in the light of the ghastly events which had led up to 1914. This was *never* to happen again! It should also be remembered that they figured very strongly as evidence of the Laws of Peace at the Nuremburg trials of 1945; laws which the Nazi leaders had violated at their personal peril. So the treaties and pacts and resolutions were by no means empty phrases. They represented the world's first genuine attempt to outlaw war.

Light from Locarno

The League was thus building bulwarks of peace, brick by brick, always searching for alternatives to armed conflict. But the most talked about achievement in its day was the Locarno Pact of September, 1925, which led directly to Germany's joining the League. The Locarno Treaty was a regional pact drawn up outside the League's normal meetings at a picturesque Swiss lakeside resort, but it was part and parcel of the same trend to outlaw war. It committed the signatories in several separate agreements, Britain, France, Germany, Italy, Belgium, Poland and Czechoslovakia to all-round disarmament, in accordance with Article 8 of the Covenant.

Lord Grey, a former British Foreign Minister, had explained the connection between disarmament and security thus:

'Bear in mind that there is no security as long as Germany is disarmed and under obligation to remain disarmed while her neighbours remain armed, and are under no obligation to disarm . . . As long as Europe is a great powder magazine, people will not feel comfortable simply because the various Governments have agreed they won't put a match to it. Nothing will make real security except to remove the powder magazine.'

But Locarno went further. Under the Treaty, Germany and France renounced the right of war as a means of altering the frontiers between them; Britain and Italy bound themselves to *guarantee* the France-German frontier and promised to help either party in case of aggression by the other. All disputes were to be settled by League procedures.

The Locarno Treaty was a big stride in the direction of security, as the French conceived it. As a result of the Treaty, Germany entered the League. 'At Locarno,' said Aristide Briand, 'we spoke European, a new language which we all ought to learn.'

The admission of Germany was the high-water mark of 1926. *It made a life-long impression on the youthful mind of the present writer, who was present at the League's Seventh Assembly, when it happened.* We can pass over the unhappy earlier events of March of that year, when a special session of the League had been called to admit Germany; but quarrelling between several aspirants to the League Council — Brazil, Poland and Spain — had prevented a unanimous vote of the Council approving Germany's admission, seeing that Germany was expected to be admitted, too, as a permanent member of the Council.

On the morning of Wednesday, September 8, on the unanimous vote (48) of the Assembly, Germany was declared by its President, Momtchilo Nintchitch of Yugoslavia, to be a member of the League of Nations. It was not until Friday morning, however, that the German delegates arrived in Geneva and took their seats at the desk marked 'Allemagne'. The Assembly Hall was packed with delegates and their staffs, the Visitors gallery was resplendent with the leading literary and other public figures of Europe and beyond. Mrs. Woodrow Wilson was among them. It could have been her late

Aristide Briand

husband's day of triumph, had he lived, for at last it seemed that some of the worst injustices of the Versailles Treaty had been corrected.

Through the open doorway there appeared, to the accompaniment of salvos of applause, the thick-set figure and close-cropped head of Gustav Stresemann, the German Foreign Minister, followed by his two colleagues von Schubert and Gaus. The President uttered a few sentences of cordial welcome and then, amid another outbreak of applause, Dr. Stresemann mounted the platform. His address was delivered in German and filled every corner of the hall. The greater part of the audience could follow little until the French and English interpreters got to work, but the event spoke louder than the words uttered. The German delegate emphasised the claims of the future, rather than dwelling on the past. He pledged Germany's resolve to co-operate in all things with the League, calling for the strengthening of the Permanent Court, international disarmament and the lowering of economic barriers. Germany, he asserted, had naturally been hostile to the League, but had slowly become converted: 'now the German Government could speak for the great majority of the German race when it declares that it will wholeheartedly devote itself to the work of the League of Nations.'

In immediate response, Aristide Briand slowly mounted the platform steps, as an astonishing outbreak of applause saluted him. Stresemann had read his speech; the French Foreign

Gustav Stresemann

Minister spoke without a note. Could the reconciliation of that day — Briand asked — have been possible without the League? Could any scene be more moving than the spectacle of former foes, while the battlefields were still crimson, meeting in that atmosphere of concord to exchange common pledges of co-operation in the work of universal peace? The orator played again and again on the words: *'c'est fini'*. 'Ended,' for France and Germany, the long succession of bloody encounters with which every page of their common history had been stained. 'Ended,' war between the peoples! 'Ended,' the long veils of mourning over sufferings that will never heal! Each had known how to show its heroism on the field of battle. Each had reaped there a rich harvest of renown. But, henceforward, 'we seek other victories in other fields.'

'So long,' declared M. Briand, 'as I have the honour to represent my country in this Assembly, the German delegates may be assured of finding a loyal collaborator in me.' Only one condition need be laid down. If Stresemann came to Geneva simply as a German, and he himself simply as a Frenchman, accords would indeed be hard to reach. 'If we come here — without losing sight, of course, of our native countries — if we are here as citizens sharing in the universality of the aims of the League of Nations, all will work out for good; our spirits will find harmonious contact with those of our colleagues in this unique atmosphere of Geneva.'

Those who came to Geneva, concluded M. Briand amidst a further tempest of applause, must leave any militant spirit behind them. If the League were to become a battlefield, where at all costs national prestige had to be maintained, then all would come to ruin. That was the road of blood, the road of the past, the road of death, of flame, of bereavement, of ruin. 'Henceforth our road is the road of peace and progress, and we shall build up greatness for our countries by leading them to lay aside their pride, to sacrifice certain of their ambitions in the service of world peace.'

On that bright and warm Friday morning in September, 1926, the world had listened to a double declaration of faith (printed verbatim in the Assembly Journal for all to read) which could well have marked the turning point in the period between the two World Wars towards the League's ultimate goal of a warless world. But words needed to be translated into *deeds.* Too soon — within half a dozen years — both Briand and Stresemann were dead; and the enemies and betrayers of the League began to take over.

Outlawing war

The League was moving towards its finest hour. Aristide Briand carried his initiative further, with Britain and Germany as his warm supporters. On 6 April, 1927, the tenth anniversary of the entrance of the United States into the First World War, the French Foreign Minister proposed that France and the United States use the forthcoming renewal of a Franco-American Treaty of 1908 as the occasion for negotiating an agreement outlawing war between the two countries. Briand's idea led to the Pact for the Renunciation of War , which was eventually signed by no less than fifteen states in Paris on 27 August, 1928. It was opened to all nations. The Geneva spirit had resulted in the co-operation of the United States, whose negative attitude had been so detrimental to a workable collective security system. American co-operation with the League was thus stimulated in many other ways during the next decade.

Sometimes called the Briand-Kellogg Pact (H. F. Kellogg was then U.S. Secretary of State), this epoch-making document called for 'uniting the civilized nations of the world *in a common renunciation of war'*. It consisted of only two articles:

> *Art. I.* The High Contracting Parties solemnly declare that they condemn recourse to war for the solution of international controversies, and renounce it as an instrument of national policy in their relations with one another.

> *Art. II.* The settlement or solution of all disputes or conflicts of whatever nature or of whatever origin they may be, which may arise among them, *shall never be sought except by pacific means.*

The Briand-Kellogg Pact came into force as world law on July 24, 1929. By 1936 it had been accepted by 65 States. Though this Pact was negotiated outside the League, like the Locarno Treaties, its origin and its support by popular opinion, owed nearly everything to the League's continuing educative work. The Pact was a plain simple statement not to go to war, which anyone could understand. It bound the United States and Soviet Russia, as well as nearly all the League members (Argentina and Bolivia did not sign). War in the future could break out between States only if one or more of them refused pacific settlement.

Between the U.S.A. and the League the Pact had built a bridge. In fact, the United States itself initiated a positive policy of 'putting teeth' in the Pact, in case a State should break the Pact. This was known as the Stimson doctrine (August, 1932), and was re-stated in 1933 by Mr. Norman Davis, then U.S. Disarmament Ambassador to the Geneva organisation. The United States had now accepted the principle of consultation with the League in the threat of war. The U.S. Government promised that, if they agreed on the facts of the aggression, they would not hinder the League's collective action against the aggressor. This was, at least, a step forward. (Both Japan in Manchuria and Italy in Ethiopia, became the first aggressors to violate the Pact, as described in Chapter 7.)

To renounce war was not, however, the invention of the authors of the Kellogg Pact. For the Covenant itself (Article

10) laid down: 'The Members of the League undertake to respect . . . as against external aggression the territorial integrity and existing independence of all Members of the League'; and (Article 13) 'The Members of the League agree . . . that they will not resort to war against a Member of the League which complies' with any award or decision. And so forth. What the 1928 Pact did was to make the prohibition absolute and binding on the signatories and bring the United States into the arena as a champion of world law. As the saying was at the time: it filled the gap in the Covenant.

Critics of the Pact — and they were many — derided it as a piece of paper hypocrisy. But there were longer-term views of the Pact's place in world affairs. One constitutional historian has described it as follows:

> Magna Carta was constantly violated by Plantagenet, Tudor and Stuart Kings; some articles of the American Constitution have remained a dead letter to this day; yet no-one would deny these acts an honoured place in the annals of human progress. The time may come when such a place will be accorded to the Briand-Kellogg Pact.[3]

As proof of its validity, the Pact played a basic role in the Nuremberg Judgments of 1946, condemning the Nazi war criminals. The Tribunal declared: 'The solemn renunciation of war as an instrument of national policy necessarily involves the proposition that such a war is illegal in international law; and that those who plan and wage such a war, with its inevitable and terrible consequences, are committing a crime in so doing.' Nor should it be forgotten that the Pact is *still* the law today.

Disarmament in sight?

We must conclude this chapter with a sketch of the most troublesome and frustrating question ever to come before the League. It was one to which it never found an answer — DISARMAMENT. We have already quoted Lord Grey, the

---

[3] Peter Price: *Power and the Law* (Geneva) 1954.

British Foreign Minister's warning in 1914: 'The enormous growth of armaments in Europe, the sense of insecurity and fear caused by them — it was these that made war inevitable.'

Several events had happened since 1914, however, which might have brought some hope to the world's peoples that a suicidal arms race need not be resumed. One thing was obvious: the World War had proved that competitive arms did *not* give security to anyone. Another thing was (as we saw in

« ... Les murs de la « Bavaria », cette brasserie pittoresque et animée, chère à M. Stresemann, s'ornent de profils lestement enlevés que soulignent de piquantes légendes, accueillies avec joie par le public et avec bonne humeur par les victimes elles=mêmes ... »

Le Temps, 20 sept. 1928.

the last few pages) that a series of agreements had been laboriously worked out to provide collective security in the place of national armaments. And the third thing was that, in the Peace Treaty itself, Germany was forced under strict supervision to cut down its soldiers and arms and fleet and military budget to a point which the victorious allies themselves agreed was 'consistent with national safety'.

Most important, the Peace Treaty laid down that German disarmament was to be followed by that of the victors. This was something quite new in world affairs. The victors solemnly declared their intentions to the vanquished as follows:

> The Allied and Associated Powers wish to make it clear that their requirements in regard to German armaments were not made solely with the object of rendering it impossible to resume her policy of military aggression. They are also the first step towards the reduction and limitation of armaments which . . . will be one of the first duties of the League of Nations to promote.

No pledge could be clearer than that. It was repeated whenever disarmament was discussed. But, in spite of the security pacts, which all contained undertakings to disarm, the pledge was never honoured. Some of the political pretexts and self-justifications for this miserable failure on the part of the victors are to be found in our later chapters. But there were deeper psychological reasons as well. Senor de Madariaga, one-time head of the Disarmament Section of the Secretariat, reasoned as follows:

> It is hopeless to try to solve the problem of armaments in isolation from the remaining problems of the world . . . We are in the presence of two facts, national armaments and wars, which are but two manifestations of international life in its present stage of development: just as individual armaments and duels are manifestations of national life in a certain stage of its development.[4]

---

[4] S. de Madariaga: *Disarmament* (Coward-McCann) 1929.

Madariaga wrote these words in 1929; yet they could hardly be more appropriate *today* as we look back at the problems of the League. The enemies are different, but the fears and fallacies, the pretexts and the motivations are the same. That is why a study of the League is so deeply disturbing, even if enlightening, today. It was never strong enough politically or spiritually to hold in check the suicidal armed rivalries of the national units which composed it, which gave it lip-service but precious little loyalty. The League lacked the dynamic force of an enlightened world opinion — a topic we shall pursue further below. As Madariaga again said: 'Duelling and the disarming of individuals had to wait till the national state was strong enough to organise the political and judiciary life of the country.' The League was like that, it never had time to organise the political and intellectual life of the world community behind its endeavours. What the late Dag Hammarskjold used to call 'world loyalty' was never powerful enough to supersede the rival local loyalties which looked to massive weapons to protect their countries against each other.

The "bloody traffic"

Instead of denigrating the League, therefore, we should appraise fairly some of the early attempts the League made to control and limit the world's armies and navies before the next terrible crisis of fear fell upon the earth. The League undertook, in fact, the first scientific study of the arms problem ever attempted. It concentrated its best brains and most devoted servants for many years upon it. It was the only international body which continuously explored this vast complex, bound up as it was with private profits and with centuries of practice of whole civilisations. In every country many civilian and military experts and important sections of the public became aware of the real problems of disarmament for the first time. It was a heroic attempt to reverse the trends of man's long history of organised warfare.

Of the two methods of approach to this problem, the indirect method we have already seen in the security pacts. 'In the present state of the world' ran an Assembly resolution in 1922, 'many Governments would be unable to accept the responsibility for a successful reduction of armaments unless they received in exchange a satisfactory guarantee of the safety of their country.' For example, under the Protocol Scheme of 1924, every State was to submit to arbitration any dispute and to accept the verdict given. Any state which took up arms rather than submit to arbitration was a common enemy. Economic and, if need be, military action would be taken by all League members against it. But this procedure was never spelled out and was only to take effect after a Disarmament Conference of all nations had adopted a scheme for the general arms reduction. Thus, security and disarmament issues were interlocked. But the Protocol became merely a historic fiction when Britain turned it down.

The direct method was seen in arms limitation conferences. The first of these was the Washington Naval Conference, which met from November, 1921 to February, 1922. Its object was to bring about a reduction of naval armaments between five countries, U.S.A., Britain, Japan, France and Italy, thus putting an end to naval competition. Great Britain, U.S.A. and Japan agreed to scrap seventy vessels. This was a good beginning, as practically the whole of Germany's navy had gone to the bottom of the sea. But was this beginning ever followed up?

In 1925, the Assembly created a Preparatory Committee for a World Disarmament Conference, which included all members of the League Council, together with Germany (not then a member), the U.S.A. and eight other States. Two weighty sub-committees, one of naval, military and air experts, the other of industrial and economic experts, were formed. However, the First World Disarmament Conference did not meet till 1932, so we shall deal with it in the next Part of this book. During these years of incubation, a stream of proposals from all countries came in on how to disarm — each other — too numerous to be summarised here; but the national arms budget grew and grew and 'security' was as elusive as the rainbow.

Meantime, we can conclude this survey by noting two directions of attack by the League: the private manufacture and trade in arms and the use of prohibited weapons. As regards the first obstacle to world disarmament, the earliest League committee set up to examine the arms traffic reported in 1921, when the memories of the recent war were still so sharp and League committees were less mealy-mouthed than they since became. The Committee asked: 'The Covenant recognises that the manufacture by private enterprise of munitions and implements of war is open to grave objections — so what *are* these objections?' Then they boldly announced: 'It is common knowledge that the public mind is strongly prejudiced against the uncontrolled private manufacture of munitions and implements of war, and it is a common belief that wars are promoted by the competitive zeal of private armament firms, and would be rendered less frequent were the profit-making impulse brought under control or eliminated altogether.' These objections to untrammelled private manufacture included:

(1) Armament firms have fomented war-scares and persuaded their own countries to adopt war-like policies and increase their armaments.

(2) Armament firms have attempted to bribe government officials, both at home and abroad.

(3) Armament firms have disseminated false reports concerning the military and naval programmes of various countries to stimulate armament expenditure.

(4) Armament firms have sought to influence public opinion through the control of newspapers in their own and foreign countries.

(5) Armament firms have organised international armament rings through which the armament race has been accentuated by playing off one country against another.

Naturally, this report was violently resented and opposed by the arms manufacturers, who replied that far from harming

Deux Familles   Two Families

Il faut choisir : bouches à feu...
ou bouches à nourrir !

Look, Mother, how well fed these are !

the world, they helped it by giving employment, paying for
research, and by discoveries such as tensile steels, rustless
metals, and trackless vehicles which are useful for peace purposes. All of which was true, of course. But the Great Debate
had begun. Scandal after scandal came to the surface in
Geneva, such as the arch-type figure of war-mongering, Sir

Basil Zaharoff, who had large holdings of munitions on *both sides.**

Similarly, the 1927 Coolidge Conference on Naval Disarmament furnished several notorious cases of war-scares . False reports abounded and its failure was due to a blank fog of mistrust, spread by rumours among the press, while America was on the edge of a huge cruiser-building programme. A Senate inquiry of 1929 tracked much of this senseless bitterness among the powers to the activity of an agent hired to attend the Conference by three big American steel and shipping firms. So the plague of the 'bloody traffic', as it came to be known, spread across the twenties. The League was powerless against these New Leviathans, the traffickers in death.

Another Geneva Convention defined who were the legal purchasers of arms, and it sought to secure publicity for the manoeuvers of the trade. Producing countries were pledged only to sell arms on an order from the importing State, under a licence. The signatory States were pledged to publish a statistical return of their foreign trade giving the 'value and the weight or number of the articles exported.' If this Convention had been universally adopted, it would have prevented arms being sold to anyone but governments. It was signed by the Great Powers, including the United States, but even by 1934 it was not in force. Thirteen States had ratified, including Britain and France, but not the United States. Was it the *League* that had failed?

A horrifying potential

As regards the second roadblock, the League published in 1924 another report, based on scientific studies supplied by the leading chemists and bacteriologists of all countries, giving the public a preview of what the horrors of chemical and biological war in the future might be like. Consequently, a Conference on the Supervision of the Trade in Arms was convened

---

* These scandals would seem to have been paled into insignificance by the gigantic bribery and corruption operations of such armament manufacturers as the Lockhead corporation in the later 1970's!

and many countries signed a Convention — the much discussed 1925 Protocol — prohibiting chemical and biological warfare.

The protocol received 37 ratifications, including Britain; but it contains a proviso which robs the pledge of much of its value. No state will deprive itself of such a weapon, however cruel, in a life-and-death struggle. So the States continued to subsidise research in the poison gases they engaged not to employ.

This bold declaration can, again, be seen as foundation stone for our own times. For in 1969 the British Government, as a signatory, presented to the United Nations Eighteen-Nation Disarmament Conference in Geneva a draft Convention, which would outlaw completely the production or use of biological methods of warfare (BW). The Convention called for a complaints procedure and investigation machinery through the U.N. The sponsors say: 'The aim of this Convention is to reinforce the 1925 Geneva Protocol (the major arms control agreement existing in this field) which forbids the use of chemical and biological methods in war by prohibiting also the production of biological agents for hostile purposes. It would outlaw completely a form of warfare which, although never used in modern times, has a horrifying potential for the indiscriminate destruction of human life.'

At the same time, the U.N. Secretary-General issued in July, 1969, a world-wide appeal against preparations for chemical and biological warfare. The *New York Times* commented as follows: 'In transmitting the work of the fourteen distinguished scientists who drew up the U.N. report, Secretary-General U Thant appealed to all states to accept the Geneva Protocol of 1925, renouncing the use of chemical and biological agents — a declaration ratified by sixty nations *but not by the United States.*' By 1975, however, most states had signed the Protocol, including the United States.

Have the nations which are still promoting the Cold War yet caught up with the old League? Or is it not clear that the League, far from being behind us, is still ahead of us? Disarmament was never in sight in the 1920's. But is it in sight in the 1970's?

"Security"?

PART III

YEARS OF FRUSTRATION

(1930-33)

CHAPTER 6

The World Crisis

"I venture to think that modern economic life is seen much more clearly when, as here, there is an effort to see it whole."
— *John Kenneth Galbraith (The New Industrial State)*

By the end of the 1920's the League stood at the zenith of its prestige and usefulness. It had disappointed the jeremiads of its severest critics. It had weathered early storms and had handled successfully, as we have seen, many political emergencies that had threatened the peace of the world. Its technical services, originally thought to be merely incidental to the League's political functions, had grown right out of proportion to the intentions of the drafters of the Covenant.

A similar sense of achievement pervaded its sister body, the International Labour Organisation. This was summed up by that dynamic Frenchman, Director Albert Thomas, in his report for 1929:

> It is impossible to conclude this annual survey of the working of the Organisation without feeling a certain optimism . . . It can now be said that the Organisation has, so to speak, reached that stage of smooth, easy running which is a common phenomenon with good motor-cars after they have done several thousand miles. The engine is 'run in'.

But the opening of the 1930's was to sound the death knell of the League. Blow after blow fell upon it. Outwardly, there was

"The League stood at the zenith of its prestige . . ."

still little sign of the threatening world crisis. The corridors of the Secretariat hummed with the comings and goings of statesmen, diplomats, experts, journalists and students of international affairs from all parts. (Among the last two was the present author.) More and more national leaders were coming regularly to the Annual Assemblies at Geneva. The spirit of Geneva had come to mean the promise of a new world order.

The long sad story of frustrations and disappointments was, however, about to begin. The first writing on the wall appeared at an inconclusive conference held in Geneva in the Spring of 1930, for the purpose of planning economic co-operation. The obstructions presented by nation after nation in framing even a loosely-worded agreement on what to *do* was an early symptom of the sickness which the League had contracted under the worsening economic depression.

To follow chronologically the course of this chronic illness from 1929 would be to multiply the length of this book a thousand times. Libraries have been written on the world crisis . But a whole generation has since grown up which is almost

1929.   Outside Assembly Hall. Philip Noel-Baker and Cecil Hurst (Legal Adviser to H.M. Government)

totally ignorant — except by mere hearsay — of the terrible impact on the life of their own forebears of the economic depression of the early thirties.

'Up to 1929 the world was relatively prosperous. Why?' asked Sir George Paish, Financial Adviser to the British Treasury. He continued: 'Because America in particular was supplying vast amounts of capital and banking credit both for home and foreign purposes. These amounts were far greater than at any time in the world's history, except in time of war. From 1924 to 1929 the American banks gave new credit to their customers of, roughly speaking, 600 million pounds ($2,500,000,000) a year. Then it became obvious that the world, including America, was over-borrowed. Everybody was out of his depth.' [1]

But this over-borrowing was only one facet of the universal catastrophe. Our account is necessarily confined to the effect of the crisis on the fortunes of the League. Yet something can be gathered in the following pages of the sense of shock and despair which settled on the world's peoples as a whole when this cyclone, starting in the United States, swept across the earth with gathering fury. Life was never to be the same again for anybody. Worse, it shattered the League and its promise of a new world order. On that League rested man's chief hope for peace and prosperity. It is most important, therefore, to understand exactly what happened, though the task of simplification is not an easy one and much that is significant must be left unsaid.

The war debts tangle

We must again turn back and recall that the First World War ended in a maze of international debts such as the world had never seen before. These colossal war debts became not only a source of friction between the United States and Europe, but one of the chief obstacles to European economic recovery. During the 1920's the debts hung like a millstone around the neck of Europe. By 1932, fourteen nations had made it clear

---

[1] G. Paish: *Problems of Peace* (O.U.P.) 1933.

that they could make no further payments to the United States unless the amounts still due were drastically cut.

We cannot here go into the reasons why U.S. domestic policies kept the foreign debtors on the hook; but we must devote a page or so to explain the relation between the *debts* due to the United States and the *reparations* demanded from the defeated Powers. For a long time the official policy of Washington — since the U.S. itself had not claimed any reparations — was to insist that debts and reparations had to be dealt with separately and apart from each other. But payments between countries are quite different from payments between individuals. In fact, in dealing with international obligations, payments to a country may often be a mixed blessing. It may even be positively harmful for a creditor country to be paid what is due to it. Let us look further into this dilemma.

The ability of the European debtors to pay and the capacity of the United States to receive war debts payments was not a question of simple arithmetic, but a question of *how* to do it. When the time came, after the First World War, for the repayment of war debts, this did not mean a flow of *money* from abroad into the pockets of U.S. citizens. With international payments, the money usually stays where it is, because each country has its own kind of money, its own currency. Foreign currencies are of little use to the other country, except to buy foreign goods with it. Since the money has to stay where it is, it is the goods that move. They moved to the debtor country to help fight its war and then back again to repay the debt. In other words, we export and import goods instead of the money.

But what about gold? Hasn't that been a medium of international payment from times immemorial? Small debts between countries can, it is true, usually be adjusted by the actual shipment of gold. But there are two reasons why gold plays only a minor role in settling international debts. In the first place, there is not enough of it. The total amount of monetary gold in the hands of both private individuals and governments in Europe in the 1920's was less than one-fifth of the total war debts. In the second place, each country kept a reserve of gold as a basis for its own currency. If that gold were drained away, its paper currency would become worthless. This happened to Germany's currency in 1923; its economic life was paralysed. Unlike individuals, countries exchange goods, not cash.

Nonetheless, only by having the two accounts — in terms of figures — offset against each other, can international payments be made. This is called the 'balance of payments'. If a foreign government wants to make the U.S. a payment, it will go to some bank where foreign exchange is bought and sold and try to buy American dollars. These dollars are usually in the form of bank credits in the United States, which can be turned into American money. But the foreign government pays for these American dollars by giving up some of its own bank deposits. As you will see, this is extremely difficult to do, unless enough Americans desire to exchange *their* dollars for foreign money, to pay for what they have bought abroad. Hence, if payments flowing out of the United States are not equal to payments flowing into the United States, the foreign governments will *not be able to buy American money,* for the

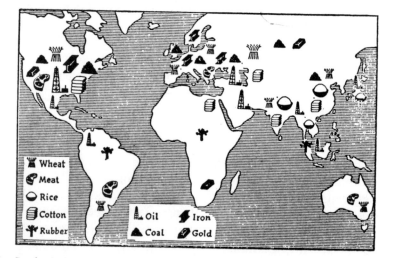

Goods which every nation needs come from all over the globe, but their free movement was blocked in the 1930's by the mounting trade barriers.

simple reason that no-one is offering American money for sale.

So the war debts could be paid to the U.S. only in such goods or services which the U.S. wanted. But did the United States, after the war, want repayment in goods and services? In general, the answer was 'NO' ! It would have meant that the U.S. must import more than it exported, and do this year after year so long as the debt payments ran. And if the U.S. imported more than it exported this would have meant a complete reversal of American expanding industry. Imported articles from debt-ridden countries would have competed with home-made articles and so diminish the sales of American products. This would also have added to the already oversupply of unsold goods. It would lower prices, reduce wages, and throw men out of work. In fact, to avoid this very dilemma the United States had long followed a policy of keeping out foreign goods, by placing a high tariff on them. For this obvious reason and many others as well, the war debts incurred by the fighting allies, could *not* be repaid after the war — even with the most honest intentions on the part of the debtors to do so.

But there was a further complication. How did these particular debts arise? During the war, the European belligerents needed huge credits to carry on a war economy and to buy munitions; they were compelled to borrow from abroad to pay for food and war equipment they bought from abroad. But these loans were advanced in the form of credits, as we have noted, and were used by the borrowing countries primarily to pay for goods bought in the United States. So the money never actually left the United States; it passed into the hands of the American business interests from whom the Allies had bought supplies. The actual cash cost of the First World War has been estimated at over *186 billion dollars,* which worked out about half the entire national wealth of the United States.

Apart from Britain, which had been a creditor to the United States until 1917, the U.S. was in a unique position at the end of the war as creditor to all the war-racked world. Physically, too, the U.S. was the major country on the allied side entirely to escape military devastation. (The same unique situation was repeated, as it happened, after the Second World War, too.)

Worse still, from the debtors' point of view, sales to the allies were made at the high level of war-time prices. Profits of American industry on them often ran as high as eighty per cent, according to the (then) Secretary of the Treasury. The United States Government raised many of these loans in turn by borrowing from American citizens through the sale of Liberty Loan Bonds. The internal public debt of the U.S. Government rose from about a billion dollars in 1916 to over 25 billion dollars in 1919. Moreover, nations which had borrowed during the war continued to get additional credits after the Armistice in 1919 for reconstruction purposes.

Hence, when peace returned, the question arose as to *how* to repay the war debts? Britain sent a mission to Washington in 1923 to negotiate a settlement of its war debts, and other governments followed. By 1930 the terms of repayments of all the debts were arranged — with the exception of the Russian war debt, since the Bolshevik Government was too desperately poor to pay foreign debts and had repudiated the Czarist war policy anyway. The total to be paid by all the European debtors under these debt agreements amounted (including interest) to 22 billion dollars. But no provision was made by Washington for a reduction of payment in the light of future changes in European economic conditions. In fact, the payment of 5% interest, as originally agreed, would have resulted in a net *profit* for the United States Government over the 62-year period that the repayment was planned to run.

So much for the basic debt figures. But a bigger problem, to which we turn, came to the fore under the heading of 'capacity to pay'. And that brings us to the question of reparations.

Road to bankruptcy

The United States Government maintained that there was no legal connection between war debts and reparations. From the world economic angle, however, the debt problem could not be settled apart from the reparations due from the ex-enemy countries. The physical devastation in Northern

France, for instance, was unimaginable; whole cities and railroads had to be rebuilt from scratch. The ex-Allies left no doubt as to their own view of *their* rights. The reparations were the sums, as we have seen, which victorious nations hoped to exact from their defeated opponents in payment of damages. Under the terms of the Versailles Treaty, Germany was given no alternative but to accept responsibility for 'causing all the loss and damage to which the allied and associated governments and their nations have been subjected as a consequence of the war imposed upon them by the aggression of Germany and her Allies.'

But *could* Germany pay these sums to the Allies, remembering the problems of transfer that we discussed above? The Treaty had left the *total* sum of the reparations to be worked out by a Reparations Commission. The Commission eventually fixed German obligations at about *32 billion dollars,* to be split between the various allied govern-

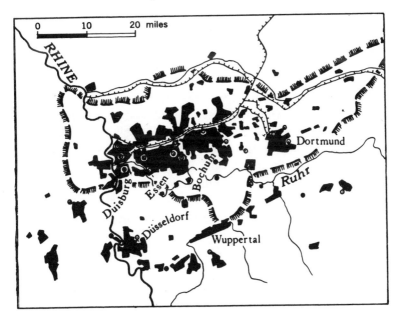

The Ruhr was the most productive coalfield in Germany. In 1923 the French invaded it, but the German miners went on strike, so production stopped.

ments. This enormous sum — more than thirty-two times the indemnity exacted by Germany from France after the war of 1870 — was recognized by many competent economists to be far beyond Germany's capacity to pay.

Not surprisingly, in 1923, Germany defaulted on some reparations deliveries of wood and coal. France and Belgium then occupied the entire Ruhr area, the country's industrial heartland. The Ruhr is the largest and most productive coal field in Europe; it contains the greatest variety of types of coal and supports the most powerful concentration of iron and steel industries on the Continent. This crude and ill-timed invasion, though legally defended by the French, was well described as an attempt to dig coal with foreign bayonets. As always with military interventions, the results came out differently from what the generals expected. The German Government proclaimed a policy of passive resistance. The coalminers struck, the factories closed, the railwaymen stopped work on French-occupied lines. Violence and bloodshed followed.

Economic hardship eventually broke the passive resistance movement. But the pressure on the Reichsmark was so great that inflation became a mad gallop. One U.S. dollar had been worth 18,000 Reichsmarks in January, 1923; by the end of the year, the dollar was worth 40,000 million Reichsmarks. A few speculators grew rich. But vast numbers of ordinary people lost their entire savings and with them their social status and self-respect. Germany's financial structure collapsed under the strain. Various insurrections, stimulated by the French — *including Hitler's* — were put down with difficulty. It was a miracle that Germany survived as a united state.

This calamity in the centre of Europe threatened the economic stability of all Europe. A committee of financial experts, under the chairmanship of Charles Dawes of the United States, was called together to work out a temporary solution. The Dawes Plan was put into effect in September, 1924, but did not challenge the total sum of 32 billion dollars fixed by the Allies that was still owing.

The Dawes Committee left Germany's total liability indefinite, but stipulated a regular *annual* payment of a little over half a billion dollars. This large sum was to be paid year after year for an unspecified period of time, based on Germany's capacity to pay. The Dawes Plan provided, however, for a large foreign loan to Germany. (This was like Peter paying Paul!) In 1929, a second committee of experts, under the chairmanship of Owen D. Young, another American, drew up a permanent plan for future reparations payments. The Young Plan is too complicated to be discussed here; but the annual payments were lower than under the Dawes Plan. Under the Young Plan, Germany was to pay *27 billion dollars,* as principle and interest, over a period of fifty-nine years. (That would bring us to 1988.) These are facts that help to explain the Second World War.

It is important to note that the reparations payments to be made each year by Germany to the ex-Allies, under both the Plans, were more than enough to cover the latter's war-debt payments to the United States. This meant that, as far as arithmetic goes, the debtors *could* pay all their war-debts out of Germany's reparations. But this pleasant make-believe was really too good to last. In fact, from 1919 to 1931, Germany made her reparations payments regularly (except in 1923 and 1924 when her economic life was paralyzed, as we have seen). And, likewise, until 1931 the ex-Allies did pay *in full* all the instalments due to the United States.

This was a period of illusion because Germany's payments between 1918 and 1921 were largely in the form of the sale of German-owned property abroad and movable equipment, such as steamships, railroad cars, and ocean cables. By giving up these capital assets, however, Germany reduced her future capacity to pay. Then followed the Ruhr period of total collapse, and after 1924 deliveries-in-kind met with strenuous objections on the part of the receiving nations. (The British found, for instance, that German coal deliveries to the French Government diminished the sale of British coal to France.) Depleting her resources thus, brought the German mark down to only a *trillionth* of its former value. This was once again inflation with a vengeance! To make things worse, Germany was not able to earn currency by a surplus of exports over imports on account of ever mounting foreign tariff barriers around her. Her exports were never enough even to pay for her imports. In a real sense, therefore, Germany had not really begun paying at all.

The evil day — the moment of truth for everyone — had been pushed off and off because of American mounting prosperity and American loans, until the blow fell. As long as Germany continued paying reparations, the payment of war debts to the United States continued. This was a vicious circle. The ex-Allies merely passed on their reparations receipts to the United States. At this time of boom, in fact, American investors were loaning more dollars abroad than the war debtors were paying into the U.S. Treasury.

There had also arisen, since the war, a still larger volume of *new* private debts owed by the German states and industries to American and other foreign bondholders. So the war debts were really being paid by private American investors — the thousands of people and firms scattered through the country who owned German bonds and so on. Thus, the United States had avoided the difficult problem of receiving vast quantities of foreign goods and services, with their own threat of serious damage to protected American industry. So the economic merry-go-round continued.

The blow falls

It was at that point of spurious and self-deceiving counter-balance that in 1929-30, the economic blizzard struck America. It then swept across the planet, leaving devastation and confusion in its tracks. Governments fell — including the British Government — the universal gold standard collapsed, and world trade dropped to a third. It was not noticed at the time that the world crisis wrecked the League beyond repair. Many later critics of the League's political collapse ignored its economic causes, which were *fundamental* to everything else.*

---

* American writers in this field usually avoid this blind spot in their studied cynicism; Elmer Bendiner's *A Time for Angels* (Knopf) 1975, is a case in point, and is true to its sub-title: "A Tragicomic History of the League of Nations."

The Dawes and Young Plans, on which stability in Europe rested, fell apart. German economic life, creeping back to 'normal', was completely disrupted by the world-wide depression. Taxes had been drastically increased; unemployment had risen until one out of every four men was out of work. Germany had become a bad investment. Foreign loans and credits, on which Germany had relied, just disappeared overnight. The 'flight from the Mark', as it was called, lowered the value of the Mark and economic chaos again spread across Germany, and beyond.

Payment of more reparations had become impossible, as everyone could see. As a result, payment of war debts just stopped dead. Faced with this realistic situation, President Hoover proposed in June, 1931, a year's moratorium or postponement of *all* inter-governmental debts and reparations. But the chain-reaction continued unabated. For example, British banks had large credits frozen in Germany and this caused a 'flight from the pound' — somewhat similar to the earlier 'flight from the Mark'. Britain was forced off the gold standard. Poorer countries faced worse calamities. This led to a heavy drain on American gold reserves. One thing was clear: the financial inter-dependence of modern nations was an inescapable fact of life. A world economic crisis called for a world economic remedy. But did it get it?

This was a God-given opportunity for the League to act as a world forum and a global clearing house. A *world* economic crisis had buffeted all nations alike, causing internal disruption which no one nation — not even the United States — could control by national action.

But did national leaders combine their efforts through the one world organisation that actually existed to cope with such a disaster? No! They were never ready with a global answer to a global challenge. In looking *inward* to their own devices, national statesmen showed themselves to be incapable of coping with their own problems, because only by *world* co-operation could their own countries be saved. This was where the Second World War really began.

The League Economic Committee's Report on 'The Present

Phase of International Economic Relations', published in September, 1935, gave a belated and negative reply:

> 'The economic *malaise* has been heavy upon the world for nearly five years. Everywhere the doctors — individuals and Governments — are at work. Unfortunately, and much against their own will, each of them is still compelled to concern himself with the cure of the malady separately from that of his neighbour . . . It has so far been impossible to attack the disease in the proper way — i.e. *internationally*.'

The world's tragedy was not basically the crisis itself, but rather (as the foregoing League report stated) 'the inability of the countries to co-ordinate their several efforts to emerge from the crisis.' In 1932, when production had reached its lowest point, the machinery of international trade was badly jammed. Tariff barriers to block out foreign goods were shooting up all around. But with the slow recovery of production, the jam became worse. 'No country deliberately desired or wished for this state of things,' lamented the same League report. 'All regretted it, all submitted to it reluctantly. But each was compelled, when the moment came, as a means of avoiding worse things, to take part in creating this situation. High duties, foreign-exchange quotas — all these succeeded one another as so many natural reflex actions in the process of self-defence . . . Each nation was compelled to take its own path; and once they were embarked on it, the different paths began to diverge. They were in fact no longer masters of their own economic policy.'

This was the story of armaments all over again; this time they were economic ones.

The League's dilemma

Summing up the foregoing events, we come to three conclusions: first, the military war had produced in due time an economic war; second, this economic war was world-wide in scope; and, third, the League was unable to deal with it. The world famous economist, John Maynard Keynes, had assailed the statesmen of the Peace Conference for their failure to apprehend 'that the most serious of the problems which claimed their attention were not political or territorial, but financial and economic, and that the perils of the future lay not in frontiers or sovereignties, but in food, coal, and transport.' [2]

A dangerous spiral of events had now begun. The depression of the 1930's had revealed the weakness of the Western powers, and gave the green light for the appearance of extremist governments in Europe — Fascist and Nazi. Democracy had obviously failed. Fearful of Communism, ordinary people were drawn to support those who promised to restore the old-style economy, while protecting them from Communism. Both Communist and Nazi parties grew in size and vigour. Both political ideologies collaborated in attacking and finally destroying the Weimar Republic and what had been the beginning of German democracy.[3] Good middle-of-the-road Germans thought that their only saviour would be Adolf Hitler.

Meantime in the United States, the depression had stimulated the election of Franklin D. Roosevelt, who was compelled to give all his attention to domestic affairs. He gave no help to the London Economic Conference which was called in 1933, to deal with the basic problems and attempt to set up a new world economic order. The London Conference was not the first of its kind. In 1927 — prior to the Wall Street slump — the League experts had *foreseen* the crisis and convened a World Economic Conference. The delegates represented many countries — officials, bankers, employers, Trade Unionists, Co-operative Societies, independent economists, Chambers of Commerce, and so on. They agreed that the world's economic ills were directly traceable to the great political and psychological dislocation left by the World War, which had affected all areas of human life.

The 1927 League Conference had achieved a wide measure of agreement as to the economic policies that *ought* to be

[2] J. M. Keynes: *The Economic Consequences of the Peace* (O.U.P.) 1922.

[3] See R. M. Watt: *The Kings Depart,* The Tragedy of Germany (Simon & Schuster) 1968.

President Titulesco.

pursued. It was most emphatic in its condemnation of high tariffs, quotas, subsidies, exchange controls and other national obstacles to international trade. But the big mistake was to insist on trying to move back to pre-war conditions. The past was a dead albatross around the necks of the sinking crewmen.

At the Assembly in September, 1929, the world depression was the main topic. M. Titulesco, the President, pointedly declared:

> The Eleventh Assembly of the League will be called upon to discuss questions exceeding in importance any with which the League has yet to deal. Any failure to solve them may involve a severe setback to the civilization of the world.

British Foreign Secretary, Arthur Henderson, stressed the urgency for *action*. 'There is a growing opinion,' he said, 'that the economic problem cannot be effectively dealt with except on an international basis. The events of recent months have demonstrated more clearly than ever that the *world is an economic unit,* that national action is impotent in itself to deal effectively with the causes of world depression.' And so on and on. More to the point, Mr. Hymans of Belgium declared: 'Some decision must be reached ... We must choose between a policy of economic isolation and nationalism or the adoption of a bold programme of economic reapproachement.'

What did the national leaders do? Nothing but talk. Meeting

Outside Assembly Hall in 1929. Arthur Henderson (Foreign Secretary) and Mrs Henderson. Behind him are Fridtjof Nansen and Philip Noel-Baker.

in July, 1933, as we noted, the London Monetary and Economic Conference made the last frantic effort to induce the countries to adopt programmes of collaboration and solidarity, based on the League's findings. But the outcome was pathetic. The drive towards economic self-sufficiency was unabated. Attempts to justify it on the theoretical grounds were plentiful and well applauded. Nationalism had won the day. The League was by-passed and ignored when it came to action.

The League had arrived before its time. No adequate world-wide effort to tackle the economic requirements of peace was made until *after* the Second World War. At last, the United

M. Hymans of Belgium arrives at Assembly.

States — more powerful than ever — took her proper part in rebuilding the shattered earth. The economic and financial leaders of the then victorious powers had met at Bretton Woods, New Hampshire, in July, 1944. In sharp contrast to the League's futile efforts, ten years earlier, the spirit of Bretton Woods has been described as follows:

> The driving impulse of the meeting, its vital and propelling force, was an overriding sense of purpose . . . to rescue the world economy, racked by chronic monetary instability and currency disorders and bedeviled by excessive trade barriers, and exchange restrictions, multiple currency practices, and barter deals during the inter-war years, and set it on the road toward the beckoning goals of broad-

based prosperity, of full employment, and of rising living standards.[4]

With the advantage of hindsight we can complete this account of the League's impotence by recalling that many intelligent observers were perfectly aware of what was happening. Martin de Traz, the Swiss authority, can be taken as typical. He pointed out in 1935 that 'towards the end of 1929 the world's economic machine lost its equilibrium . . . In vain has the League offered its services and its methods. It is no longer heard, for its programme is in complete contradiction to the economic policy of each of its members.'[5]

In the following chapter we shall explore what resulted in the field of military operations leading up to World War II. But can anyone today disguise the fact that the self-centered and competitive policies of the inter-war period destroyed the very organisation on which the peoples of the world depended for their common safety and prosperity? Each government continued trying to pull itself up by its own bootstraps. No-one succeeded.

As a final gesture, an experienced European economist and former Prime Minister of Belgium was invited to conduct an inquiry into remedies. In 1938, his report — the Van Zeeland Report — stated: 'The isolated, divergent and contradictory measures by which the nations attempted to protect themselves against it, and push off the burden on to their neighbours, have only served to precipitate it and to render it yet more grievous for all.' Mr. Van Zeeland proposed a World Trade Pact for all nations to join, pledging themselves to economic collaboration and to tackle point by point the obstacles to an open world trade programme.

Alas, 1938 was far, far too late! The Ides of March had already come.

What was missing?

When one looks back on this confused story of how the nations of the world got into such a mess over their accounting

---

[4] B. K. Madan: *Finance and Development* (Washington, D.C.) No. 2, 1969.
[5] M. de Traz: *The Spirit of Geneva* (O.U.P.) 1935.

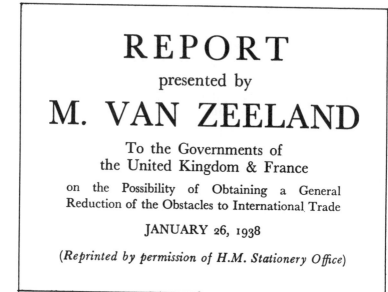

REPORT

presented by

M. VAN ZEELAND

To the Governments of
the United Kingdom & France

on the Possibility of Obtaining a General
Reduction of the Obstacles to International Trade

JANUARY 26, 1938

(*Reprinted by permission of H.M. Stationery Office*)

problems, the natural question is 'WHY'? Everything was there that *could* be produced or transported — trains and skills, minerals and plantations. In fact, coffee and wheat were actually being burnt or dumped into the sea in some countries, while ships rotted in the harbours and millions starved. What was basically wrong?

The printing presses have since turned out book after book in a score of languages; countless politicians have since made thousands of speeches trying to explain *why*. Somehow a common theme seems to run like a *leitmotif* through all these explanations. The world's peoples — millions and millions of ordinary citizens — had backed their national governments in running the world into disaster after disaster; but they still backed their national governments in making the disaster worse. Will it ever be possible on this earth for them to institute and support a *world* programme instead? The Geneva organisation was there to help them do this; but it demanded the sort of spiritual commitment which they were not ready to undertake. Leaders and peoples lacked the *will* to use the

League as *their* League, their way of life, their salvation. In the race between education and disaster, disaster had won.

In concluding this Chapter, however, let us examine further what we mean by 'education'. More than one statesman was heard to say at Geneva: 'I would myself like to support this or that programme of common action, BUT the people behind me are not behind me!' This is how a distinguished professor of International Relations at Oxford expressed it at the time: 'It is not the function of the League to impose Geneva standards upon reluctant or refractory peoples.' And he continued:

> The ordinary citizen of a modern state understands his own immediate interests and those of his country or region or professional group better than he understands, or can ever be expected to understand, their interaction with the interests of other countries and of the world as a whole . . . Why should he consent to walk in step with the rest of the world until it has been made clear to him that both the discipline and the objective of the march are worth his while?[6]

One criticism of the League of Nations was that it was actually a League of Governments. A plan was in fact considered at Paris which would have given the League not only a Council and an Assembly, but also a Congress *directly representative of the peoples themselves*. This third body was — alas! — omitted from the League's constitution. But the idea found expression in the creation of unofficial citizens' groups, linked together at Geneva by the International Federation of League of Nations Societies. The Federation's aims were expressed thus:

> The success or failure of the League *depends on public opinion*. If the people of the world want the League to succeed, then the League will succeed. No Government in any country will dare to oppose the League if the public opinion of that country wishes to support it, nor will any Government support it if public opinion wishes to oppose it.

---

[6] A. Zimmern: *The League of Nations and the Rule of Law* (Macmillan) 1936.

For example, British men and women who wanted the League to succeed formed themselves into such a national society called the League of Nations Union. At its highest point the League of Nations Union registered half-a-million paid-up members and organised thousands of public meetings and demonstrations and published a continuing stream of publications. Likewise, in the United States the League of Nations Society did yeoman service in supporting and publicising the League, as well as in maintaining lively lobbies in both Washington and Geneva.[7] Similar groups existed in Canada, France, Germany, and elsewhere.

The spirit and uphill work of these voluntary societies was reflected in the following quotation from a Federation statement: 'The art of war has been taught from the beginning of history. The inevitability of war, even the desirability of war has been preached throughout the ages. Now for the first time the art of peace and the desirability of peace are being taught on an organized basis. If there is to be a League of Nations, there must be public opinion behind it. If there is to be public opinion behind it, there must be League of Nations Societies. If the societies are to do their work with maximum efficiency, they must be joined in a Federation.'

Annual congresses of the Federation were held in different world capitals. Representative and well-known public figures from fifty or more countries worked together to put the League in a position to do its job. For, as Sir Alfred Zimmern insisted: 'By itself it is nothing. Yet the peoples persistently regard it as Something . . . But that Something does not reside in a tabernacle at Geneva. It is communicated to Geneva by the peoples of the Member States. It is their will and their will alone which can make the League a living reality.'

As we have shown, the world was not yet ready for the spiritual change in people's minds which the League demanded. Yet, as part of this new direction, a small committee of the world's leading servants and academic leaders was set up in Paris with the honorific title of the Committee for

---

[7] See Clark Eichelberger: *Organising for Peace* (Harper & Row) 1977.

Intellectual Co-operation. Its quiet and intensive work for international education may not have made big headlines at the time, but from this small League brains-trust there was founded, immediately following the Second World War, the United Nations Educational, Scientific and Cultural Organisation (UNESCO), which nowadays has become a household word and global force.

From its Paris centre UNESCO has promoted a vast range of some of the most promising worldwide educational and scientific enterprises of our time. It has salvaged the rich treasures of the Lower Nile Valley and the priceless art galleries of Venice, plumbed the depths of the Indian Ocean for edible proteins to feed undernourished millions, and built and equipped thousands of schools and trained countless teachers and educators throughout Africa and Asia. Again, it was the League that led the way, and today, at last, is justified of her children.

Lord Cecil (U.K.), Motta (Switzerland), Albert Thomas (France) at laying of foundation stone of Palais des Nations.

CHAPTER 7

Roots of Aggression

"The first, and almost the only, question we put to our-
selves when with a critical eye we examine this strange
international parliament, is this: 'Is it capable, in case of
conflict, of imposing a peaceful solution?'"

— *André Maurois*

As we saw, the Economic Conference which the League
sponsored in London to help resolve the World Crisis led to
nothing.

The Disarmament Conference which had opened in Geneva
in 1932, after years of preparation, produced no tangible result.

When the League sought to mediate between China and
Japan, it failed to prevent war; Japan left the League rather
than accept its verdict.

Such are the lamentable set-backs which the League encoun-
tered during the brief period in the mid-30's that we shall
examine in this Chapter.

Germany broke away and began to re-arm, at first in secret,
then openly. She transformed herself into a gigantic munitions
factory. The other nations, who had never fulfilled the pledge
given in the Treaty to disarm in like measure, seized on Germany's re-armament as an *extra* incentive, as it was, to re-arm
themselves more rapidly. The arms race was on — once again.

It is true that the departure of Germany and Japan was
counterbalanced by the admission of Russia, but the League
was never the same again. We have entitled this Chapter Roots
of Aggression , because we must look below the orthodox and

Arthur Henderson, one-time British Foreign Secretary, opening the Disarmament Conference in 1932.

often one-sided accounts which the press and politicians gave their peoples at the time. The true causes of the breakdown of world peace, which preceded the Second World War, cannot be condensed in a general term like 'Nazi aggression'. They are worthier of deeper study in a situation so profoundly inter-mixed as the one we have just described. Let us look closer.

Disarmament fails

After five years of preparation, the First World Disarmament Conference, with Arthur Henderson, Foreign Secretary
of Britain, in the chair, opened in Geneva on February 2nd,
1932. On the bright side, this Conference differed markedly
from previous diplomatic Conferences by reason of the
obvious pressure of public opinion upon it in its initial stages.
A great number of national as well as international
organisations, representing millions of ordinary men and
women, came to Geneva to express their anxious desires to the
delegates by means of pleas and petitions in favour of disarmament.

A premonition of pending disaster was in the air. The
petitions contained millions of signatures, collected in a score
or more of countries, including the United States and Britain.
It was the biggest international demonstration, up to that date,
to put an organised public sentiment behind the League's
superhuman attempt to cut down the world's mounting
weapons of death. A representative deputation organised by
the two major international associations of war veterans and
ex-servicemen and a strong deputation led by Lord Robert
Cecil on behalf of a number of international organisations
were received by the President of the Conference. Hundreds of
thousands of telegrams, messages and resolutions from
religious and civic groups and voluntary societies all over the
world were received at intervals and recorded in the daily
journal of the Conference.

On the dark side, one of the symbols of the coming demise of
the Conference might be seen in a prank played on the
assembled delegates by some outsider one morning when,
behind the Chairman's seat, two *identical* military rifles could
be seen affixed to the wall; each had a label in French beneath
it, one reading 'This is a *defensive* weapon' and the other 'This
is an *offensive* weapon'.

With great subtlety and logic the Big Powers brought forward scheme after scheme to disarm *each other,* while the
smaller powers looked on supporting one plan or another

Ramsey MacDonald.

according as they felt their own security would be strengthened. But the military advisers of each government always had plenty of reasons why nothing should be done by themselves.

Later in 1932, Russia (not yet a member of the League), Italy and Germany called for all-round disarmament of *any* kind, provided it was begun at once and included every country. The United States proposed a one-third cut for everyone in stages. The Conference resolved to accord to Germany 'equality in principle', as laid down twelve years earlier in the Peace Treaty. As Prime Minister of a coalition government in Britain, Mr. Ramsay MacDonald's rich Scottish accents, so well-known within the British Labour ranks he had deserted, fell like a soothing rain on the parched and anxious audience, who had come to Geneva's second home, *Le Bâtiment Electoral,* as the one centre where mankind could erect a common defence against war and want, if they chose to do so.

But, in 1933, finding no hope of concessions *in practice,* and following close on Hitler's election as Reich Chancellor, Germany left the Disarmament Conference and resigned from the League. Incidentally, that same year the British Minister of Air (Lord Londonderry) publicly congratulated himself on blocking a resolution to abolish air forces. So Germany was not alone in osbtructing the Conference. In 1934, Hitler announced the re-establishment of the German air force and increases in the navy — a direct violation of the Versailles

Treaty. In 1935, Germany re-introduced conscription, again in violation of the Treaty.

Further details of the many plans submitted to the Conference would be futile here, though it should be remarked that Russia was admitted to the League in 1934 and at once pressed for drastic all-round disarmament under League supervision. After four years of anxious and intense debate the Conference was suspended, but not closed. If the results of its work had fallen so far below the high hopes entertained in 1932, this did not mean that the League's work had been wasted. The principles on which the various delegations could be said to have reached agreement would be found invaluable for a practicable guide to real measures of disarmament in a political atmosphere less charged with explosiveness. Technically, the experts working at the Conference had proved that universal arms reduction was *possible*. It was the political rivalry, backed by the military vested interest, which blocked the way.

The Conference had made progress in two ways, however. It was agreed in principle to organise, in case of threat of war, consultation between all States, provided an armaments convention were first concluded. It was also agreed in principle to prohibit aerial bombardment and the use of chemical, incendiary, and bacteriological weapons, on the basis of the 1925 Protocol, noted above. But these agreements were never put into a formal Convention.

Several explanations were current in thoughtful circles in the West for these grave and disappointing results. One was a natural scepticism about the League's ability to replace existing national armaments by a world system of *collective* security. Another was — so obvious from the record of these years — the prevailing nationalistic attitudes and egotisms which had turned the League into a mere debating society. But perhaps a more profound explanation was that the Disarmament Conference was bound to fail because so many of the Governments represented at it were the willing tools of their arms manufacturers and allied commercial interests, who were determined on rearmament schemes as their best means of ensuring economic and social survival from the conditions created by the slump. The records of the early 1930's show that war preparations became an integral and necessary part of the process of recovery from the same world depression featured in our last chapter as the death-knell of the League.

Japan invades

In contrast to the slow attrition of the Disarmament Conference, the blow which Japan struck at the League was swift and sudden. Though we can only skirt the main questions of Far Eastern aggression here, we can at least note three episodes that led to Japan's quitting the League.

The first phase takes us back behind the scenes of the Paris meeting in early 1920. The Peace Conference would seem to have brought Japan, at long last, into the framework of the sophisticated Western world. But Professor Alfred Zimmern notes a psychological impasse which developed at the Conference which had a most significant bearing on later events. He states: 'Grave as were her economic preoccupations, something else, graver still, was on her mind. She was haunted by the problem of race relations. For four centuries the white man, by his mastery of the arts of power, had been hammering into the mind and spirit of the non-white peoples the conviction that they were his natural inferiors. The Russo-Japanese War had indeed demonstrated that this supremacy could be challenged in the field of battle. But the stigma still remained.' [1]

The Japanese delegate moved the following resolution which, however, never reached the stage of discussion:

> The equality of nations being a basic principle of the League of Nations, the High Contracting Parties agree to accord, as soon as possible, to all alien nationals of States members of the League, equal and just treatment in every respect, making no distinction, either in law or fact, on account of their race and nationality.

The second phase of Japan's relations with the West was, of course, the collapse of world markets, on which her

---

[1] A. Zimmern: *League of Nations and the Rule of Law* (Macmillan) 1936.

burgeoning industries depended. It was more than a co-
incidence that the three military autocracies of Japan, Germany and Italy, should have followed so soon in the wake of
that crisis. The structure of Japanese finance and industry was
particularly vulnerable to outside influences. The family
banking houses of Mitsui, Mitsubishi, and Sumitomo (the Big
Three) held a quarter of Japan's finance capital, while five
more firms held another quarter. That is to say, half Japan's
industrial capital was in the hands of these eight firms, which,
in close association with the Satsuma and Chosu landowning
families of the old feudal aristocracy, supplied all the Navy and
Army officers and practically controlled Japan's public life.
Even more so than in Europe, the distress arising from the
world slump became the basis of intensive rearmament.

Thus an Army-Big-Business dictatorship — an industrial
military complex — swiftly grew, which launched the Man-
churian adventure in 1931. This military adventure managed to
silence internal discontent for a time; it gave a profitable investment for Japanese capital, as well as jobs for the generals. But it
had two dire results: it committed Japan to war preparations
that pressed ever harder on the low standard of living of the
Japanese people, and it made an implacable enemy of China,
thus isolating Japan more from the world as a hostile neighbour. This was the real beginning of the 'surprise' attack on
Pearl Harbour ten years later. Pearl Harbour symbolised the
West's downgrading of Japan's struggle for supremacy in the
Pacific.

The third phase came just before an emergency meeting of
the League Council, called under Article 11 of the Covenant,
when China appealed for help on September 21, 1931, following the occupation by Japanese troops of Mukden and other
places along the South Manchuria Railway. China begged the
Council to take steps to restore the *status quo ante* and to
determine damages. The Council appealed to the two Governments to refrain from acts which might aggravate the situation
and demanded the immediate withdrawal of the invading
troops. The United States expressed official sympathy with the
Council's attitude. A representative of the United States sat at

the Council meetings, since the Briand-Kellogg Pact was obviously being violated. Although the Council noted Japan's assurance 'that it has no territorial designs in Manchuria,' it could do nothing to avert the aggressive military operations by Japanese forces, including the aerial bombardment of various cities, which China reported had taken place.

The Japanese aggression continued. A British journalist, one-time editor of *Foreign Affairs* and an official delegate to two of the League Assemblies, stated with unusual frankness: 'Japan, watching the insolence of Europeans towards China in the throes of a slow revolution, concluded that China would not be able to rely on any sure help from the League of Nations, should Japan intend some day to renew her absorption of further portions of Chinese territory. The invasion of Manchuria in 1931 did not have its origin in that year.' [2]

Following a fact-finding Mission of Inquiry sent to the Far East, under a British statesman, Lord Lytton, the League convened a special meeting of the Assembly the following March. But nothing tangible was done nor could reasonably be done by the League, partly due to the fact that Russia and the United States, the Powers who were disposed to take a firm stand against Japan, were not League members; also that the two most powerful League members, France and Britain, were hesitant in their attitude. France would not go beyond moral disapproval, while the policy of the British Government was frankly pro-Japanese. Behind the British policy of benevolent neutrality was the reluctance of industrial and financial interests to apply economic sanctions that might jeopardise their investments in Japan.

Japan then announced that Manchuria had decided to become independent of China under the name of Manchukuo , with the generous aid of Japanese officials. In other words, Japan had annexed Manchuria as her economic colony. (Did not the other Great Powers in the League own colonies, gained by military action in the past?) In response to the League's almost unanimous paper condemnations, how-

---

2   H. M. Swanwick: *Collective Insecurity* (Cape) 1937.

Japan takes over Manchuria, 1931-33.

ever, Japan gave on March 24, 1932, the required two years' notice of withdrawal from the League.

Both Council and the Assembly had presented a unanimous verdict that Japan was the aggressor, that the sovereignty of Manchuria remained with China, and that no member of the League should recognise 'Manchukuo'. No member did. But, alas! the aggressors were neither checked nor appeased. In 1937, the major attack on the mainland of China was resumed — another prelude to the Second World War, as far as the Far East was concerned. It is easy to forget how the democratic nations of the West left China at the mercy of Japan.

Germany quits

A detailed account of what went wrong in Germany under Hitler cannot be given here, but three important stages in the devolution of the German problem as it affected the League can be listed as follows: (1) Internal disruption; (2) Violation of the Treaty; and (3) Resignation from the League.

First, a modern authority on Germany — a German citizen living in Germany at the time — has well summed up his country's internal disruption as follows:

> 'The twenty-six years between the signing of the Versailles peace treaty in 1919 and the end of the Second World War were a period of almost continuous political, economic and social upheaval in Germany. In retrospect, it seems as if the Democratic Republic that followed the armistice carried at birth the seeds of its own destruction; so great were the strains and stresses to which it was exposed.' [3]

We have noticed some of these seeds of destruction already — the tyranny of reparations, the invasion of the Ruhr, and the continuous inflations and subversions and revolts (including Hitler's). At the bottom of all lay the loss of human dignity, which plays a primary part in nation-building or in nation destruction. Since 1919, an Allied army of occupation remained on the right bank of the Rhine. The disarming of Germany was supervised by groups of Allied officers, who naturally met with every kind of passive resistance. Yet they eventually reported that the Treaty stipulations had been carried out. However, the volunteer army of 100,000 men, allowed Germany under the Treaty, became the best organised in all of Europe, efficient, dedicated, and capable of swift expansion. The high command went underground and the civilian Government turned a blind eye to evading the Versailles Treaty whenever it could. It should be remembered, moreover, that against the Government were pitted the sworn enemies of the Weimar Republic, chief among whom were the Nazis and Communists, as well as the frustrated militarists. They all collaborated in destroying the Government, thus preparing the way for the Second World War.

In spite of this, as Professor Walton states: 'The five years of calm between 1924 and 1929 gave Foreign Minister Gustav

[3] Henry Walton: *Germany* (Walker & Co.) 1969.

Stresemann, the outstanding statesman of the Weimar Republic, a chance to restore German standing in the world community and to try to alleviate some of the hardships of the Versailles Treaty.' We have described this as Stresemann's policy of 'fulfilment'. Unquestionably it had begun to work for the benefit of Germany and world peace, following admission of Germany into the League in 1926. Awarded the Nobel Peace Prize for his work of European conciliation, Stresemann had nonetheless to face all the time the vicious abuse of uncompromising nationalists who considered every step he took as a sell-out to foreign interests. He died of a stroke in October, 1929, spiritually and physically an exhausted man. But even on his death-bed he negotiated the evacuation of the Rhineland by the Allied forces for an earlier date than laid down in the accursed Treaty.[4]

Second, although clandestine violations had constantly occurred, they had not been substantial ones during the policy of 'fulfilment'. When Stresemann passed away in October, 1929, amidst the rancour of his enemies, the Geneva of Locarno had come to an end. With the advent of Hitler to supreme power in 1933, the treaty violations began in earnest. This is not to say that the Germans did not believe that they had reason on their side. Here is a facsimile of the telegram of the German Foreign Minister (Baron von Neurath) sent to Geneva on 14th October, 1933:

> 'On behalf of the German Government I have the honour to make to you the following communication: In the light of the course which recent discussions of the Powers concerned have taken in the matter of disarmament, it is now clear that the Disarmament Conference will not fulfil what is its sole object, namely general disarmament . . . This renders impossible the satisfaction of Germany's recognised claim to equality of rights. The conditions on which the German Government agreed at the beginning of this year again to take part in the work of the Conference thus no longer exists. The German Government is accordingly compelled to leave the Disarmament Conference.'

---

4   See A. Vallentin: *Stresemann's Race with Death* (Constable) 1931.

Third, Hitler undoubtedly had the sentiments of the German people as a whole with him when, on the same date, he declared (not for the first time): 'By the deliberate refusal of real moral and material equality of rights to Germany, the German nation and its Governments have always been profoundly humiliated.' Later on in the same speech, the newly-proclaimed dictator asserted:

> "The German nation is not in a position, as an outlawed and second-class nation, to continue to take part in negotiations which would only lead to further arbitrary results. It will therefore also announce its departure from the League of Nations."

Russia joins

It has been the object of this book to look at this crucial twenty-year period, 1919-1939, not from the point of view of the English-speaking world alone but, above all, from the perspective of the League, as representative of the attitudes and aspirations of its fifty or so members. We have so far tried to show how it looked from inside the League. In 1917, Russia had undergone a permanent revolution and had made its own peace settlement at Brest-Litovsk with (then) undefeated Germany. The Bolshevik Government was not even invited to the Paris Conference.

Long before Russia was admitted into the League in 1934, however, Soviet delegations had attended various League and related Conferences, already mentioned. There can be no doubt, on the record, that the Leninist Government had put forward proposal after proposal for drastic all-round disarmament. Yet none of these proposals seemed to have got anywhere. The Soviet Union was, in fact, the first nation to ratify the Briand-Kellogg Pact. It is interesting to note, for instance, that in 1932 the Soviet Union backed the U.S. plan for a cut of a third in all armaments.

'The fact that Lenin called the League of Nations a "thieves' kitchen" has been used as evidence that the Soviet Union was not sincere in its entry into the League,' once stated a well-known authority on the Soviet Union: 'it was not adverse to associating with capitalist Governments individually and found no objection to associating with them collectively, when it thought that this action would promote the cause of world peace.'[5]

From the League's point of view, both the Soviet Union and the United States had contributed to bring on the Second World War by their isolationism. Outside events had forced this policy on Russia; but the United States deliberately chose isolation by renouncing both the Versailles Treaty and the League of Nations. Steadily, however, it could be seen that United States and League interests coincided more and more closely as the years passed. The Soviet Government had taken no part in the Paris Conference, as we have seen; and it certainly had no interest in maintaining the 'capitalist' peace settlement — until it was almost too late. Soviet leaders were not eager to become involved in foreign adventures in view of their defeat in 1917 and the foreign interventions in their country by the Allies following the First World War. Communist propaganda had meantime stirred up suspicions and distrust of Soviet policies in Europe. Western leaders on their side were never eager to work with their opposite Communist numbers, and much of the League's struggle to devise universal collective security met with no concrete support in Moscow.

But when the Soviet Union joined the League in 1934, it soon began to call for steps to halt 'Fascist aggression'. Yet it seemed that Stalin was at the same time seeking to make a deal with the new Nazi leader, Adolf Hitler, as Stalin had no faith whatsoever in the democratic League. The Soviet view was that the conclusion of a non-aggression treaty with Germany was the only sensible step for their Government to take because, in the autumn of 1939, the Soviet Union had problems with Japan as well as with Germany. 'War threatened the Soviet Union on two fronts,' said the official historian, 'in Europe and in the Far East. And, besides, the Soviet Union was without allies and fully isolated.' The Soviet Government had to ensure the

---

[5] Andrew Rothestein (Tass News Agency Correspondent) in *Problems of Peace* (Allen & Unwin) 1937.

national security of the U.S.S.R. to save the country and the people from the approaching danger. So it would appear that Russia had no more faith than Germany in the League. In 1941, in spite of their pact, both were at each other's throats in a life and death struggle.

The League now seemed to be back at the stage of the robber barons of the Middle Ages or the rival princes at the times of Machiavelli. And into this clash of nationalisms had been imported the conflict of ideologies. It was all a disastrous retreat back from a stability, security and peace that had never, in fact, existed. It had been completely overlooked that the Spirit of Geneva also was an ideology — a way of life. When the nations chose to leave the League or by-pass it or give it lip-service, as they did do, they lost more than the neglected League, they lost the fragile peace.

The Psychology of Armaments.

PART IV

YEARS OF DECLINE

(1934-1939)

CHAPTER 8

Dragon's Teeth

"There was nothing wrong with the Covenant of the League. Its general principles were right. It formed a logical and reasonable system which should not be incapable of practical application. Its shortcomings were due to the failure on the part of States Members to apply the system loyally and integrally."
— *Anthony Eden (Foreign Secretary, 1936)*

The League had five years to live as a potential force in Europe. In this final chapter we shall point to those events which marked the last struggle of the League's supporters to keep their heads when (as Kipling would have said) 'all about them were losing theirs and blaming it on them.' But the dragon's teeth were already sown by many hands. Our earlier chapters have shown that; and the harvest of armed men now stretched right across the tortured earth.

In the Conclusion, we shall try to summarise some of the vital lessons which the League experiment has left for a new generation to ponder. Meanwhile, one result of Japanese aggression in the Far East, and the League's incapacity to cope with it, was that pro-League forces tended to fall back on Europe. The continued indifference of the United States served to enforce this trend. Throughout the 1930's, many strong voices called for a European solution beyond the illusive aim of security, as no world solution seemed to be in sight. Yet the Japanese venture had itself proved that security was either *world* security or *no* security. The dynamic Aristide Briand had already tried his hand at a European Union. He had used the Assembly platform again and again in his forensic appeals ever since Locarno. But when the Briand plan for a United Europe went into the committee stages it foundered on something more powerful than logic, namely, geography. Where did Europe end? At the Russian frontier? If not, at the Urals? Or at Vladivostok? And did it include the British colonies (then governed from London) or the British Empire (including Canada and Australia)? Did it cover the French, Dutch and Belgium colonies? And so on? Where *did* Europe leave off? Those Assembly debates would be very instructive today, if they were read by present-day advocates of a 'united' Europe.[1]

There existed in the fateful 1930's, however, a more pragmatic reason why Europe could never become a junior league on its own. Japan's resignation was quickly followed by Italy's and Germany's aggressions. The League's hands were now full with the defections of two powerful European partners, soon to be followed by Russia's expulsion. Both the former countries had ratified the Locarno Treaty against aggression and the Briand-Kellogg Pact against war itself. It should not be overlooked, however, that even if the League's impotence was becoming obvious to everyone, an even more dismal failure attended the numerous military pacts that had proliferated around the League, in flat contradiction to the League's principles. It was, in truth, these very powerful military alliances — not the weak League — that drove the nations of Europe into the Second World War. This primary fact should never be forgotten.

If the League was a fragile life-raft on the stormy seas of the 1930's, the rival alliances could be likened to the acts of drowning men struggling around the life-raft, frantically dragging each other down into the depths. When Woodrow Wilson failed in 1920 to get even to the floor of the U.S. Senate the proposed tri-partite Treaty of Mutual Guarantee between the U.S., Britain and France, two results followed, with dire

---

[1] The questions of European Union and Atlantic Union are taken up in detail in the present author's *End of an Illusion* (Allen & Unwin) 1969.

effects on the future of the League. Britain, on the one hand, rejected every form of military alliance lacking the co-operation of the U.S., and later rejected, as we have seen, the League's own Treaty of Guarantee in 1923 and the Protocol that followed in 1924. France, on the other hand, turned its security to a series of military alliances with smaller states: Belgium, Poland, Rumania, Yugoslavia and Czechoslovakia. Similarly, the new nations of central Europe, lacking sufficient man-power and industry to become powerful allies, tied themselves to each other in military pacts such as the Little Entente between Czechoslovakia, Yugoslavia and Rumania — aimed, of course, at Hungary.

Mussolini's war

A minor incident at Wal-Wal on the frontiers of Ethiopia (or Abyssinia) and Italian Somaliland in December, 1934, gave the Italian dictator a world stage on which to display his personal glory. Mussolini began to make extravagant demands on Haile Selassie's primitive but independent kingdom. Meanwhile, Italian war preparations were accelerated. Japan's aggression in China undoubtedly encouraged Mussolini to launch his attack against the Abyssinians. Japan found in Mussolini an apt pupil. The lesson was in tune with his own ambitions. Ethiopia, he argued, was Italy's Manchukuo: a source of raw materials, a territory to be colonised, and a future market.

Why did not the League act? Frightened by Hitler's rise in Germany, France hesitated to lose Italian support. British public opinion, however, was indignant and outraged and called on the League of Nations to support Ethiopia — provided Britain was not obliged to go to war. At the League of Nations Assembly in September, 1935, the British delegation led the way and promised full backing for a peace initiative at Geneva.

When Italian armies invaded Ethiopia a month later, the League actually voted sanctions against Italy, including an oil embargo. This was an historic and courageous first step for the League to take. But could these sanctions work? The French

Emperor Haile Selassie.

Benito Mussolini.

government deliberately sabotaged all efforts to enforce the oil sanctions. London and Paris then devised a plan outside the League to partition Ethiopia between an Italian protectorate and the remainder which was to become an Italian Colony. This plan became infamous and known as the Hoare-Laval Pact of December, 1935. It was not ratified because of public opposition in Britain; but the harm had been done. Mussolini went ahead and completed his conquest of Ethiopia in 1936, and sanctions were withdrawn as unworkable. The dramatic personal appeal of Ethiopia's Emperor Haile Selassie stirred the Assembly, but it did not stop the black-shirts.

This had been a test case for 'sanctions'. Guarantees had been the heart of the League problem from the beginning, as we have noted throughout these pages. The word sanctions means a penalty for a breach of the law. It is not used in the Covenant, as such; but Article 16 states that 'should any member resort to war in disregard of its covenants,' this would be regarded as 'an act of war against all other Members of the League.' In that case, 'it shall be the duty of the Council to recommend to the several Governments concerned what effective military, naval or air force' each member shall contribute to check the law-breaker. This was very drastic language. But, *before* the Council got down to this exacting task of deciding on military sanctions, *all* members of the League were committed immediately — without waiting for the Council to act — to cut off *all* trade and financial relations and prohibit *all* contracts between their own citizens and those of the war-making state.

This is what was meant by sanctions under the Covenant. They *could* be military; but they *had* in any case to be economic and diplomatic. At the 1919 Peace Conference the French had pressed for an international armed force to be set up and prepared in advance to enforce (as the saying is) the new world law. But Woodrow Wilson and the British were against a League army and navy. The Ethiopian incident seemed to many to drive home the point of the French argument: when Italy struck, nothing was ready in advance. Italian troops and arms were already going through the Suez Canal, while Britain, which controlled the Canal, was still debating the imposition of sanctions. Action on economic sanctions was improvised far too late and was too soon called off, because Italy had conquered Ethiopia before the boycott had begun to

Haile Selassie at Assembly 1937.

work. Moreover, many League members never took part in the boycott at all. The League members were, however, so disturbed by the Italo-Ethiopian war that they set up, before it was over, nearly a hundred committees and expert groups to deal with the carrying out of Article 16 'next time'. All to no purpose.

To be or not to be?

It is not proposed to summarise here all these proposals and arrangements, but for the few remaining years of the League's effective life, sanctions became the main topic of debate. Given that sanctions were morally right — and good law — *could* they, in fact, ever be put into practice by sovereign states? As we have noted, already in 1931, when Japan invaded Manchuria, League members had sidestepped sanctions against Japan as impractical. From that time on, statesmen struggled with the problem: To be or not to be?

In Britain, France, and other European countries, public opinion was divided. The United States, pursuing its isolationist policy, attempted to evade the issue, too — until, that is, Pearl Harbour in 1941 brought it onto America's doorstep. One section of opinion said: The League Covenant (Article 16) means what it says: an aggressor country must be stopped by cutting it off from the rest of the world by stopping its trade as far as possible; if that doesn't bring its government to heel, then our warships and troops must be combined as a united 'police' action to stop it. The opposite section of public opinion insisted: But that is not police action at all, that is war; the League was set up to prevent war between its members, not to conduct a war between them. Moreover, even if we don't go beyond an economic boycott, outside pressure on a sovereign state can only result in its people rallying the firmer behind their own Government. This was no easy dilemma to resolve. It has never been resolved to this day. The famous 'veto' at the U.N.'s Security Council is one legacy of that debate.

What actually happened in the case of Italy was that the League Council *did* agree in 1935 that (a) Italy was the aggressor, (b) Ethiopia was to be supported in every way possible, short of war operations, and (c) economic sanctions, including an oil embargo, were to be applied by the League members. Italy promptly resigned from the League. Britain and some other members of the Council started to carry out their undertakings. But without the United States, and with the refusal of other oil-trading nations to act, it was soon realised that theory could not be put into practice.

Are sanctions feasible?

The full implications of sanctions, as an international policy, did not come up again until — in our own time — the case of Rhodesia came before the United Nations in 1966. The United Nations condemned Rhodesia for its racist policy and agreed in almost unanimous votes of both the General Assembly and the Security Council to cut Rhodesia off from a list of important imports and exports. It set up a Sanctions Committee to work out details. This later experiment in depriving a law-breaking country of essential trade and commodities and diplomatic recognition is now in its final stages. But the subterfuges which that outlawed Government has for over ten years employed to maintain outside economic supplies, and also the devices, open or secret, that other governments or their private traders have employed to defeat the United Nations decisions, demonstrate the complexity of the problem.*

This raises the fundamental question: Will governments of sovereign states ever be mature or co-operative enough to uphold world law when it conflicts with national interests or with the private interests of their own business communities? Or are sanctions between sovereign states an anomaly, anyway? Until these primary questions can be answered today, one cannot look back critically at the League and say: It was a bad League because it failed to apply sanctions against the aggressor.

---

* As this book goes to press, the strangle-hold of economic and financial pressure on Rhodesia's illegal government has proved to be a major cause of its collapse; a primarily military solution was never within sight of realisation until African guerrilla action began.

Voting for peace

1935 was a mixed year. It saw the halls and offices beginning to rise for the new League of Nations building in Geneva, called the *Palais des Nations.* And, reverting to the dilemma which faced the nations over sanctions against Italy in 1935, it can also be recalled that British public opinion was deeply stirred at what seemed to be a growing League paralysis. This concern was reflected in a national campaign initiated by the League of Nations Union (L.N.U.) called the 'Peace Ballot'. The purpose of this carefully planned 'National Declaration for Peace and Disarmament' was to educate public opinion in support of the League during this time of trial. The ingenious method adopted by the L.N.U. and the wide range of religious and civic

PEACE . . BUT HOW?

Wolverhampton Peace Week,

October 28th————November 6th.

MANCHESTER ANTI-WAR EXHIBITION
St. PETER' INSTITUTE, Wulfruna Street.

: THE PROGRAMME :
FOR THE WEEK

Oct. 28. EXHIBITION OPENED by HIS WORSHIP THE MAYOR at 2-30 p.m.

Oct. 30. PUBLIC MEETING in St. PETER'S INSTITUTE, 8 p.m.

Speakers : MISS ELLEN THORNEYCROFT
Brig.-Gen. CROZIER,
            C.B., C.M.G., D.S.O.
CANON MORRIS.

Chairman : Rev. R. G. ELDRIDGE

Oct. 31. PUBLIC MEETING in THE MASONIC HALL, 8 p.m.

Speakers : JAMES JOYCE
J. R. CAMPBELL

Chairman : B. NEWTON BATES.

The League Headquarters "Palais des Nations", Geneva.

groups that co-operated, was to send tens of thousands of volunteer canvassers to people's homes up and down the country, and ask them to vote on five specific questions, summarised as follows:—

(1) Are you in favour of the League of Nations?
(2) Do you agree to all-round reduction of arms?
(3) Do you favour abolition of air bombing?
(4) Should private arms manufacture be abolished?
(5) If one nation attacks another, should other nations combine to stop it by—
  (a) non-military measures?
  (b) military measures?

To this remarkable nation-wide unofficial canvass, no less than *twelve million* individuals gave in their answers. Over eleven million gave 'Yes' to Question 1; over ten million gave 'Yes' to Question 2, 4, and 5a; and over nine million gave 'Yes' to Question 3. As regards military sanctions (Question 5b) there was a considerable drop; but still just under seven million

gave 'Yes' to the specific words 'military measures, if necessary'. On the other hand, over two million said 'No' to this question — far more negatives than came in under the other questions.

This unique testing of public opinion was conducted under the leadership of Lord Robert Cecil. It reminds us that the sanctions issue was not being taken lightly either in Britain or other countries during the 1930's. In essence, it was the sanctions issue embodied in the Covenant that was one of the main obstacles to the United States joining the League in the first place. The way in which the argument was presented by the organisers of the Peace Ballot was as follows:

> National armed forces exist. All the nations have decided to use force for defence. So the only question which remains is whether the League method of combining against the aggressor or the old method of allowing each to be his own defender is the less dangerous. And if you must use arms for defence, they are less likely to provoke war if linked visibly to the collective system instead of to the old political method. Arming in both cases is evil but less dangerous than the armed *anarchy,* so of the two evils we must choose the less. If arms there must be, far better that they should be put behind the law, than left in the hands of the rival litigants.

What such a ballot would bring forth today, in terms of public support for 'collective security' under the United Nations, no-one knows. The Korean War represented the only case where the U.N. has been involved directly in what can be termed military sanctions against an alleged aggressor. The ultimate wisdom of that fluke decision has since been widely disputed. Suffice, again, to say that the League had to face in the 1930's momentous issues to which we have by no means found an answer today.

Lord Robert Cecil

Hitler and Lebensraum

With the consolidation of popular support and business and military power behind the German dictator, following Germany's resignation in 1933, the worried statesmen of Europe turned their backs on the League altogether. The sombre story has been told too many times to need amplifying here. Although Stage One can be said to have been set by the German defeat in 1918; Stage Two can be put, historically and factually, with the economic crisis — by 1930 unemployment in Germany had already reached six million. Stage Three was plainly reflected in the political arena, as summarised below.

In 1930, *six and a half* million Germans voted Nazi in the Reichstag elections, and 107 Nazis took their seats in the Lower House of 646 seats. This was eight times the Nazi votes and seats in the pre-crisis election, two years earlier. Two years later pro-Nazi votes increased to over *nineteen* million, and 230 Nazis took their seats. One year later, *seventeen* million voted Nazi and 288 gained seats. This was the crucial year 1933, when Hitler became Chancellor, ordered withdrawal from the League, and demanded absolute dictatorial powers.

In 1935, as we noted earlier, the Saar went over to Germany by a peaceful and overwhelming vote, organised and policed under a League plebsiscite. But in that same year, the demilitarised Rhineland was occupied by Hitler's troops in defiance of the Treaty provisions. But this was not the end — only the beginning. In 1938, Hitler formed the Axis Pact with Mussolini, and at once took over Austria, whose territory both dictators had long coveted. Japan soon became the third member of the Axis.

Meanwhile, a cruel Civil War broke out in Spain (1936-39), between the new Republican Government and yet another dictator, General Franco, who brought in Moorish troops from North Africa. This provided both the other dictators with a European battleground. Britain and France, like the United States, decided on non-intervention; but the Soviet Union tried to help the Republican Government, mainly through a limited number of aircraft and Russian pilots. This intervention was of

From 1937 the League Council began to meet in the new Palais des Nations Council Room.

little avail. Yet in 1937 the League moved into its new imposing *Palais.*

Late in 1938, Hitler demanded that the German population of Northwestern Czechoslovakia—the Sudetens—be incorporated, like the Austrian population, into a greater Reich. In Munich, on September 29th, 1938, the British and French Prime Ministers, Neville Chamberlain and Edouard Daladier, met Hitler and Mussolini face to face and accepted the German occupation of Sudetenland as an alternative to war. But in March, 1939, Hitler took over the rest of the country.

The next and last demand of Hitler to wreck (or rectify) the Versailles settlement, before the Second World War broke out, was to abolish the troublesome Polish Corridor and occupy what had been East Prussia. When on the first of September, 1939, Poland was invaded by Germany, Britain and France both, on the third, declared war on Germany. This was not done as a League sanction, but by virtue of guarantees given to Poland under a military treaty. The Second World War had

The first meeting of Assembly met in the new (present) Palais des Nations in 1938, as war-clouds threatened.

begun. Soviet Russia at the same time occupied east Poland 'for security reasons', but did not become a belligerent against the Western allies. The United States, though giving moral and material support to Britain and France, remained neutral. The League Council and Assembly met in December, 1939, and expelled the Soviet Union for its invasion of Finland — the only time a member had been expelled.

Was the Second World War inevitable?

The foregoing factual outline is all we have space to include in a book about the League of Nations. The League and the Peace Treaty on which it was founded were unceremoniously swept aside by the makers of the nations' destinies as they led their peoples into a war which has not even yet achieved a legal peace settlement in Europe, though the Helsinki Pact of 1975 is considered to be a political settlement — exactly 30 years late!

But could this Second World War have been avoided or prevented? Thirty-seven years have passed since the lights went out all over Europe for a second time in a generation. And the historians have been at work on the archives and private memoirs and have listed the mistakes, the misjudgments, the omissions of the men in power, and the men who might have been in power, during the League's twenty years of tortured existence.

The reader must be left to his own speculations. Here are two or three 'IFS' for him to consider. If those seven crucial votes in the United States Senate had been available to President Wilson in March, 1920, *would* the League have succeeded in preventing the Second World War? Again, at Munich, in 1938, M. Daladier, Prime Minister of France, stated: 'France asked for help, but President Roosevelt's reply was "not one man, not one cent" — so we had no alternative.' What would the reader have himself done at Munich? Was Winston Churchill right when in 1944, as Prime Minister, he stated: 'This unnecessary war . . . could easily have been prevented if the League of Nations had been used with courage and loyalty by the associated nations?'

In this line of questioning have we not ostensibly been speculating on one basic theme, namely, whether strong military force behind or within the League could have saved the peoples from the Second World War? For was it not military force that finally broke the League? Can this state of affairs ever be changed? Will military force ever make possible a League — now the United Nations — which will be able to (as the U.N. Charter says) 'save succeeding generations from the scourge of war?'

In our Conclusion we shall return to this crucial question. The League's twenty years of short but eventful life, surveyed in these pages, left that question unanswered. Can the League experience help us find an answer to it today?

Three stages in the League Buildings

1920

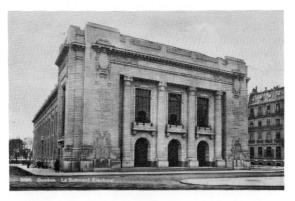

1930

1938

CONCLUSION

The Legacy left the United Nations

"Does this mark an end or a beginning? The answer, of course, depends on our perception and the action we take."
— *Charles Lindberg, pioneer flyer (at launching of Apollo 8 in 1968).*

The most important part of the League story is yet to come. But it cannot be told in this book. For we, the readers, are still writing that story. The *good* that the League did lives on after it; but — we may ask — has the *bad* been interred with its bones?

The answer to this question lies in one's attitude — or perception — as Colonel Lindberg said on watching Apollo 8 ascend into space from United States soil — where he himself had started on the first trans-Atlantic flight. If the League had been an end in itself, it ended rather badly. But if the League was part of a process, an historic evolution going back over hundreds, it may be thousands, of years, then the League was infinitely worthwhile, and well worth studying for the pioneer part it played in that process during our own exciting century.

And if the League is looked upon as a working experiment and as a necessary stage in mankind's development, then its successor, the United Nations, is also an experiment, a further stage on — to what?

It has been observed that, when the drafters of the U.N. Charter were producing the structure of the new World

Organisation at San Francisco in 1945, the speeches and discussions were noteworthy for an absence of references to the old League (still in legal existence at that date). Professor Leland M. Goodrich, an authority on the U.N., points out that this silence about the recent past was not surprising, if for no other reason than that the United States had practically ignored the League, and that the Soviet Union — now the second most powerful partner in the new organisation — had been thrown out of the League in 1939 for bad conduct. Some tender consciences must have been at work!

This is no reason, however, why the serious student should ignore the League today, insists Professor Goodrich, because: 'If his studies lead him to the conclusion that the United Nations is in large measure the result of a *continuous evolutionary development* extending well into the past, instead of being the product of new ideas conceived under pressure of the recent war, that should not be the occasion for despair. We know from the past that those social institutions which have been most successful in achieving their purposes are those which are the product of gradual evolutionary development ... While progress largely depends upon the discovery and application of new ideas and techniques, it has always been considered the test of practical statesmanship to be able to build on the past, adapting what has been proven to be useful in past experience to the needs and requirements of the changing world.' [1]

This is a particularly encouraging approach for the generation which has grown up since the United Nations was founded. It was just the point made by the U.N. Secretary-General in the message which he sent in 1969 to the International Student Movement for the United Nations, holding their world conference at Kampala, Uganda:

> To the new generation, the United Nations may alternatively appear as part of a tired establishment or as a revolutionary instrument in a search for global partnership. If the latter view is to prevail, the Organisation must

---

[1] Leland M. Goodrich: "From League of Nations to United Nations", *International Organisation* (1947), World Peace Foundation, U.S.A.

gear itself to new conditions, streamline and improve its institutional machinery, and keep its programmes and work abreast, or even ahead, of the new developments . . . If the Organisation is to continue to evolve in these directions, it will need the active support of the forward-looking younger generation everywhere.

*   *   *   *   *

Commenting on Immanuel Kant's *Essay on Perpetual Peace,* a modern political philosopher, Dr. David Mitrany, has stated that Kant did not look for a solution in any sudden moral transformation of mankind, but that, already in the 16th century, he had 'predicted that after many trials the nations would be forced to establish a federation of free states based upon the principle of voluntary assent and submission to the rule of law to save mankind from annihilation.' Dr. Mitrany records his own belief: 'Progress has been laborious, and, on the whole, unaided by political wisdom. Yet therein lies the true lesson of its story. It shows that our present experiments are not the chance product of some visionary mind. They are neither the fruit of theory nor the play of theory, but rather the highest ledge reached so far in the evolution of the Western system.' [2]

This belief that the League was an essential evolutionary stage in man's conquest of war and control of his destiny was frequently expressed during the League's lifetime by those who worked closest to it and shared its trials and frustrations. General Smuts, for instance, a pragmatic statesman and successful soldier, whom we saw hard at work on the League's foundations, once referred to it as 'the enduring temple of future world government' and 'the new organ of world government'. This advanced view implied that — one day — the League would inherit that measure of national sovereignty which formerly belonged to the Member States that composed it.

Yet, when describing the League as he saw it, General Smuts

[2] D. Mitrany: *The Progress of International Government* (Yale) 1933.

also wrote: 'Let us proceed at once to discard the idea of a super-state which is in the minds of some people ... States will be controlled not by compulsion from above but by consent from below.' This particular founding father recognised, as we have often noted in these pages, that public opinion — the people's consent — had a long, long way to go before it could accord the League (or its successor) the sovereign powers that a future world federal government would entail, to deal with questions of peace and war and the world economy, while preserving national questions for national decisions within the separate nations.

Senor de Madariaga, another devoted League servant, whom we have also quoted in this book, writing about his experience in the Geneva organisation, said bluntly: 'A club of sovereign nations is not a State.' He goes on to point the moral *why* the League was bound to fail in stopping war:

> What becomes of co-operation when one of the co-operators fails? Where is the higher plane whence the law is to draw its majesty? ... What is clear is that we are not consistent if we both want peace and refuse to recognize the World Commonwealth and block its coming by insisting on national sovereignty and by reducing the status of the Covenant to a mere contract. Peace means justice; justice means law; law means a world community conceived as an *organic unity,* i.e. a World Commonwealth.[3]

This is strong language by those who know the real price of peace: global authority over the sovereign state. For 'war' means war between sovereign states. This realisation brought a straight, unambiguous challenge from the lips of H. G. Wells, one of the most prolific commentators on *The Way the World is Going* (the title of the book from which his words are taken): 'Either you are for Cosmopolis or you are for War.'

*   *   *   *   *

---

[3] S. de Madariaga: *The World's Design* (Allen and Unwin) 1938.

On April 18, 1946, the League Assembly adjourned its final session after taking the legal steps needed to terminate the existence of the League of Nations and transfer its assets to the United Nations. On August 1, the transfer took place at a simple ceremony in Geneva. 'Thus,' records Professor Goodrich, 'an important and, at one time, promising experiment in international co-operation came formally to an end. Outside of Geneva, no important notice was taken of this fact.'

This quiet and unassuming transfer to the new World Organisation of twenty arduous years of experience and functions brings us back to the conclusion of the famous Swiss observer, when in 1935 he closed his *The Spirit of Geneva* with the words: 'Whether peoples want it or not, their destinies are now so closely intertwined that it is impossible for the League of Nations to disappear. If tomorrow some catastrophe destroyed it, it would come to life again under a different name. As Professor Gilbert Murray has well said: "The League may not be efficient, but it is certainly indispensable".'

What, then, were the traditions and basic functions that the League passed over to the U.N.? We have noted a number of these in the foregoing chapters — how, in fact, the United Nations, as a living institution, has taken over, adapted, broadened and developed a substantive range of the League's global purposes.[4] Apart from the almost universal character of the United Nations, with its 150 or more members — including the United States, as its most influential member — its highly trained and specialist staff of nearly 10,000 individuals have more than fulfilled the farthest hopes and dreams of so many of the League reformers, not least by the fact that most of the U.N. budget today and 85 per cent of its personnel are spread across the globe engaged in economic and social, educational and technological programmes. These are the real *peacemakers;* the builders of what, in League times, seemed an impossible dream. All countries, particularly the developing countries, owe much of their material progress to this massive team work. The specialized agencies and technical organs of

---

[4] See, for examples, this author's earlier works on the U.N., especially *The Story of International Co-operation* (Watts, New York) 1967.

the U.N. family have become an indispensable part of their internal economies. The current news headlines and mass media give only a distorted and fragmentary picture of this new world order.

In the area of peace-*keeping,* as contrasted with the collapse of what used to be called 'collective security', the U.N. has developed over barely a decade a series of workable non-violent techniques in peace-keeping. With a minimal use of force, U.N. observers, negotiators, and 'blue helmets', have initiated a new type of peace strategy which, as it wins wider acceptance and experience, will make today's titanic national armaments appear as irrational and obsolete as they are suicidal and futile. That there are grave and crucial lessons still to be learned from the League experiment is all too evident. For even the simplest of these lessons does not yet seem to have penetrated the minds of national leaders, namely, that the way to peace is never through war.

The League *had* to be reformed. There could be no doubt about that. Its last active days, before the Second World War, were full of plans and proposals for reforming it, from all directions. One of these reformers, Clarence Streit, an American journalist, approached the problems posed by League reform with the American experience of 1787 in mind. He stated that the American democracy got out of its problems then by reorganising interstate government. 'They reorganised by shifting the basis,' he stated, 'the supreme unit and object of interstate government was shifted from the state to the individual citizen. They began their Constitution with "We the People", and no longer with "We the undersigned Delegates of the States". It seems a small thing, this shift from State to Man — it was really a revolution, the second great American revolution — but small or great, it worked. It seems to me that is a good lead for us to follow now . . . After all, what man has done, man can do.'[5]

But can we not say today that a major step in that reform has already begun? The U.N. Charter does begin: 'We the Peoples'.

[5] C. Streit: "Reform of the Covenant is not Enough", *The League and the Future of the Collective System* (Allen & Unwin) 1937.

And, in the thirty years of its career, a sense of global citizenship, even world loyalty, has been developing among some leaders, its personnel, and countless supporters in country after country. That is why a comparison with both the theory and practice of its predecessor is so important today.

By looking back we can mark the progress not only of institutions, but of the men who shape them. A new breed of men is evolving within and through and around the World Organisation, whose chosen vocation is to make this earth a true home for man. They have dedicated themselves to the same tasks that the League began but left unfinished.

It has been said that when a star breaks it gives birth to a thousand suns. That is just what has happened with the League.

Text of Covenant

(The original text of the Covenant was approved by the Peace Conference on April 28th, 1919. The text given here is as amended in later years by the League Assembly. But the amendments were few.)

Preamble

THE HIGH CONTRACTING PARTIES,

In order to promote international co-operation and to achieve international peace and security

by the acceptance of obligations not to resort to war,

by the prescription of open, just and honourable relations between nations,

by the firm establishment of the understandings of international law as the actual rule of conduct among Governments, and

by the maintenance of justice and a scrupulous respect for all treaty obligations in the dealings of organized peoples with one another,

Agree to this Covenant of the League of Nations.

Article 1

1. The original Members of the League of Nations shall be those of the Signatories which are named in the Annex to this Covenant and also such of those other States named in the Annex as shall accede without reservation to this Covenant.

Such accession shall be effected by a Declaration deposited with the Secretariat within two months of the coming into force of the Covenant. Notice thereof shall be sent to all other Members of the League.

2. Any fully self-governing State, Dominion or Colony not named in the Annex may become a Member of the League if its admission is agreed to by two-thirds of the Assembly, provided that it shall give effective guarantees of its sincere intention to observe its international obligations, and shall accept such regulations as may be prescribed by the League in regard to its military, naval and air forces and armaments.

3. Any Member of the League may, after two years' notice of its intention so to do, withdraw from the League, provided that all its international obligations and all its obligations under this Covenant shall have been fulfilled at the time of its withdrawal.

Article 2

The action of the League under this Covenant shall be effected through the instrumentality of an Assembly and of a Council, with a permanent Secretariat.

Article 3

1. The Assembly shall consist of Representatives of the Members of the League.

2. The Assembly shall meet at stated intervals and from time to time as occasion may require at the Seat of the League or at such other place as may be decided upon.

3. The Assembly may deal at its meetings with any matter within the sphere of action of the League or affecting the peace of the world.

4. At meetings of the Assembly, each Member of the League shall have one vote, and may have not more than three Representatives.

Article 4

1.   The Council shall consist of Representatives of the Principal Allied and Associated Powers, together with Representatives of four other Members of the League. These four Members of the League shall be selected by the Assembly from time to time in its discretion. Until the appointment of the Representatives of the four Members of the League first selected by the Assembly, Representatives of Belgium, Brazil, Spain and Greece shall be members of the Council.

2.   With the approval of the majority of the Assembly, the Council may name additional Members of the League whose Representatives shall always be members of the Council; the Council with like approval may increase the number of Members of the League to be selected by the Assembly for representation on the Council.

The Assembly shall fix by a two-thirds majority the rules dealing with the election of the non-permanent members of the Council, and particularly such regulations as relate to their term of office and the conditions of re-eligibility.

3.   The Council shall meet from time to time as occasion may require, and at least once a year, at the Seat of the League, or at such other place as may be decided upon.

4.   The Council may deal at its meetings with any matter within the sphere of action of the League or affecting the peace of the world.

5.   Any Member of the League not represented on the Council shall be invited to send a Representative to sit as a member at any meeting of the Council during the consideration of matters specially affecting the interests of that Member of the League.

6.   At meetings of the Council, each Member of the League represented on the Council shall have one vote, and may have not more than one Representative.

Article 5

1.   Except where otherwise expressly provided in this Covenant or by the terms of the present Treaty, decisions at

any meeting of the Assembly or of the Council shall require the agreement of all the Members of the League represented at the meeting.

2.   All matters of procedure at meetings of the Assembly or of the Council, including the appointment of Committees to investigate particular matters, shall be regulated by the Assembly or by the Council and may be decided by a majority of the Members of the League represented at the meeting.

3.   The first meeting of the Assembly and the first meeting of the Council shall be summoned by the President of the United States of America.

Article 6

1.   The permanent Secretariat shall be established at the Seat of the League. The Secretariat shall comprise a Secretary-General and such secretaries and staff as may be required.

2.   The first Secretary-General shall be the person named in the Annex; thereafter the Secretary-General shall be appointed by the Council with the approval of the majority of the Assembly.

3.   The secretaries and staff of the Secretariat shall be appointed by the Secretary-General with the approval of the Council.

4.   The Secretary-General shall act in that capacity at all meetings of the Assembly and of the Council.

5.   The expenses of the League shall be borne by the Members of the League in the proportion decided by the Assembly.

Article 7

1.   The Seat of the League is established at Geneva.

2.   The Council may at any time decide that the Seat of the League shall be established elsewhere.

3.   All positions under or in connexion with the League, including the Secretariat, shall be open equally to men and women.

4.   Representatives of the Members of the League and officials of the League when engaged on the business of the League shall enjoy diplomatic privileges and immunities.

5.   The buildings and other property occupied by the League or its officials or by Representatives attending its meetings shall be inviolable.

Article 8

1.   The Members of the League recognize that the maintenance of peace requires the reduction of national armaments to the lowest point consistent with national safety and the enforcement by common action of international obligations.

2.   The Council, taking account of the geographical situation and circumstances of each State, shall formulate plans for such reduction for the consideration and action of the several Governments.

3.   Such plans shall be subject to reconsideration and revision at least every ten years.

4.   After these plans shall have been adopted by the several Governments, the limits of armaments therein fixed shall not be exceeded without the concurrence of the Council.

5.   The Members of the League agree that the manufacture by private enterprise of munitions and implements of war is open to grave objections. The Council shall advise how the evil effects attendant upon such manufacture can be prevented, due regard being had to the necessities of those Members of the League which are not able to manufacture the munitions and implements of war necessary for their safety.

6.   The Members of the League undertake to interchange full and frank information as to the scale of their armaments, their military, naval and air programmes and the condition of such of their industries as are adaptable to war-like purposes.

Article 9

A permanent Commission shall be constituted to advise the Council on the execution of the provisions of Articles 1 and 8 and on military, naval and air questions generally.

Article 10

The Members of the League undertake to respect and pre-serve as against external aggression the territorial integrity and existing political independence of all Members of the League. In case of any such aggression or in case of any threat or danger of such aggression the Council shall advise upon the means by which this obligation shall be fulfilled.

Article 11

1.   Any war or threat of war, whether immediately affecting any of the Members of the League or not, is hereby declared a matter of concern to the whole League, and the League shall take any action that may be deemed wise and effectual to safe-guard the peace of nations. In case any such emergency should arise, the Secretary-General shall on the request of any Member of the League forthwith summon a meeting of the Council.

2.   It is also declared to be the friendly right of each Member of the League to bring to the attention of the Assembly or of the Council any circumstance whatever affecting international relations which threatens to disturb international peace or the good understanding between nations upon which peace depends.

Article 12

1.   The Members of the League agree that if there should arise between them any dispute likely to lead to a rupture, they will submit the matter either to arbitration or judicial settle-ment or to inquiry by the Council, and they agree in no case to resort to war until three months after the award by the arbitrators or the judicial decision or the report by the Council.

2.   In any case under this Article the award of the arbitrators or the judicial decision shall be made within a reasonable time, and the report of the Council shall be made within six months after the submission of the dispute.

Article 13

1.   The Members of the League agree that whenever any dispute shall arise between them which they recognize to be suitable for submission to arbitration or judicial settlement, and which cannot be satisfactorily settled by diplomacy, they will submit the whole subject-matter to arbitration or judicial settlement.

2.   Disputes as to the interpretation of a treaty, as to any question of international law, as to the existence of any fact which if established would constitute a breach of any international obligation, or as to the extent and nature of the reparation to be made for any such breach, are declared to be among those which are generally suitable for submission to arbitration or judicial settlement.

3.   For the consideration of any dispute, the court to which the case is referred shall be the Permanent Court of International Justice, established in accordance with Article 14, or any tribunal agreed on by the parties to the dispute or stipulated in any convention existing between them.

4.   The Members of the League agree that they will carry out in full good faith any award or decision that may be rendered, and that they will not resort to war against a Member of the League which complies therewith. In the event of any failure to carry out such an award or decision, the Council shall propose what steps should be taken to give effect thereto.

Article 14

The Council shall formulate and submit to the Members of the League for adoption plans for the establishment of a Permanent Court of International Justice. The Court shall be competent to hear and determine any dispute of an international character which the parties thereto submit to it. The Court may also give an advisory opinion upon any dispute or question referred to it by the Council or by the Assembly.

Article 15

1.   If there should arise between Members of the League any dispute likely to lead to a rupture, which is not submitted to arbitration or judicial settlement in accordance with Article 13, the Members of the League agree that they will submit the matter to the Council. Any party to the dispute may effect such submission by giving notice of the existence of the dispute to the Secretary-General, who will make all necessary arrangements for a full investigation and consideration thereof.

2.   For this purpose the parties to the dispute will communicate to the Secretary-General, as promptly as possible, statements of their case with all the relevant facts and papers, and the Council may forthwith direct the publication thereof.

3.   The Council shall endeavour to effect a settlement of the dispute, and if such efforts are succesful, a statement shall be made public giving such facts and explanations regarding the dispute and the terms of settlement thereof as the Council may deem appropriate.

4.   If the dispute is not thus settled, the Council either unanimously or by a majority vote shall make and publish a report containing a statement of the facts of the dispute and the recommendations which are deemed just and proper in regard thereto.

5.   Any Member of the League represented on the Council may make public a statement of the facts of the dispute and of its conclusions regarding the same.

6.   If a report by the Council is unanimously agreed to by the members thereof other than the Representatives of one or more of the parties to the dispute, the Members of the League agree that they will not go to war with any party to the dispute which complies with the recommendations of the report.

7.   If the Council fails to reach a report which is unanimously agreed to by the members thereof, other than the Representatives of one or more of the parties to the dispute, the Members of the League reserve to themselves the right to take such action as they shall consider necessary for the maintenance of right and justice.

8.   If the dispute between the parties is claimed by one of them, and is found by the Council, to arise out of a matter which by international law is solely within the domestic jurisdiction of that party, the Council shall so report, and shall make no recommendation as to its settlement.

9.   The Council may in any case under this Article refer the dispute to the Assembly. The dispute shall be so referred at the request of either party to the dispute, provided that such request be made within fourteen days after the submission of the dispute to the Council.

10.   In any case referred to the Assembly, all the provisions of this Article and of Article 12 relating to the action and powers of the Council shall apply to the action and powers of the Assembly, provided that a report made by the Assembly, if concurred in by the Representatives of those Members of the League represented on the Council and of a majority of the other Members of the League, exclusive in each case of the Representatives of the parties to the dispute, shall have the same force as a report by the Council concurred in by all the members thereof other than the Representatives of one or more of the parties to the dispute.

Article 16

1.   Should any Member of the League resort to war in disregard of its covenants under Articles 12, 13 or 15, it shall *ipso facto* be deemed to have committed an act of war against all other Members of the League, which hereby undertake immediately to subject it to the severance of all trade or financial relations, the prohibition of all intercourse between their nationals and the nationals of the covenant-breaking State, and the prevention of all financial, commercial or personal intercourse between the nationals of the covenant-breaking State and the nationals of any other State, whether a Member of the League or not.

2.   It shall be the duty of the Council in such case to recommend to the several Governments concerned what effective military, naval or air force the Members of the League shall

severally contribute to the armed forces to be used to protect the covenants of the League.

3. The Members of the League agree, further, that they will mutually support one another in the financial and economic measures which are taken under this Article, in order to minimize the loss and inconvenience resulting from the above measures, and that they will mutually support one another in resisting any special measures aimed at one of their number by the covenant-breaking State, and that they will take the necessary steps to afford passage through their territory to the forces of any of the Members of the League which are co-operating to protect the covenants of the League.

4. Any Member of the League which has violated any covenant of the League may be declared to be no longer a Member of the League by a vote of the Council concurred in by the Representatives of all the other Members of the League represented thereon.

Article 17

1. In the event of a dispute between a Member of the League and a State which is not a member of the League, or between States not members of the League, the State or States not members of the League shall be invited to accept the obligations of membership in the League for the purposes of such dispute, upon such conditions as the Council may deem just. If such invitation is accepted, the provisions of Articles 12 to 16 inclusive shall be applied with such modifications as may be deemed necessary by the Council.

2. Upon such invitation being given the Council shall immediately institute an inquiry into the circumstances of the dispute and recommend such action as may seem best and most effectual in the circumstances.

3. If a State so invited shall refuse to accept the obligations of membership in the League for the purposes of such dispute, and shall resort to war against a Member of the League, the provisions of Article 16 shall be applicable as against the State taking such action.

4. If both parties to the dispute when so invited refuse to accept the obligations of membership in the League for the purposes of such dispute, the Council may take such measures and make such recommendations as will prevent hostilities and will result in the settlement of the dispute.

Article 18

Every treaty or international engagement entered into here-after by any Member of the League shall be forthwith registered with the Secretariat and shall as soon as possible be published by it. No such treaty or international engagement shall be binding until so registered.

Article 19

The Assembly may from time to time advise the recon-sideration by Members of the League of treaties which have become inapplicable and the consideration of international conditions whose continuance might endanger the peace of the world.

Article 20

1. The Members of the League severally agree that this Covenant is accepted as abrogating all obligations or under-standings *inter se* which are inconsistent with the terms thereof, and solemnly undertake that they will not hereafter enter into any engagements inconsistent with the terms thereof.

2. In case any Member of the League shall, before becoming a Member of the League, have undertaken any obligations inconsistent with the terms of this Covenant, it shall be the duty of such Member to take immediate steps to procure its release from such obligations.

Article 21

Nothing in this Covenant shall be deemed to affect the validity of international engagements, such as treaties of arbitration or regional understandings like the Monroe doctrine, for securing the maintenance of peace.

Article 22

1.   To those colonies and territories which as a consequence of the late war have ceased to be under the sovereignty of the States which formerly governed them and which are inhabited by peoples not yet able to stand by themselves under the strenuous conditions of the modern world, there should be applied the principle that the well-being and development of such peoples form a sacred trust of civilization and that securities for the performance of this trust should be embodied in this Covenant.

2.   The best method of giving practical effect to this principle is that the tutelage of such peoples should be entrusted to advanced nations who by reason of their resources, their experience or their geographical position can best undertake this responsibility, and who are willing to accept it, and that this tutelage should be exercised by them as Mandatories on behalf of the League.

3.   The character of the mandate must differ according to the stage of the development of the people, the geographical situation of the territory, its economic conditions and other similar circumstances.

4.   Certain communities formerly belonging to the Turkish Empire have reached a stage of development where their existence as independent nations can be provisionally recognized subject to the rendering of administrative advice and assistance by a Mandatory until such time as they are able to stand alone. The wishes of these communities must be a principal consideration in the selection of the Mandatory.

5.   Other peoples, especially those of Central Africa, are at such a stage that the Mandatory must be responsible for the administration of the territory under conditions which will guarantee freedom of conscience and religion, subject only to the maintenance of public order and morals, the prohibition of abuses such as slave trade, the arms traffic and the liquor traffic, and the prevention of the establishment of fortifications or military and naval bases and of military training of the natives for other than police purposes and the defence of

territory, and will secure equal opportunities for the trade and commerce of other Members of the League.

6.   There are territories, such as South West Africa and certain of the South Pacific Islands, which, owing to the sparseness of their population, or their small size, or their remoteness from the centres of civilization, or their geographical contiguity to the territory of the Mandatory, and other circumstances, can be best administered under the laws of the Mandatory as integral portions of its territory, subject to the safeguards above mentioned in the interests of the indigenous population.

7.   In every case of mandate, the Mandatory shall render to the Council an annual report in reference to the territory committed to its charge.

8.   The degree of authority, control, or administration to be exercised by the Mandatory shall, if not previously agreed upon by the Members of the League, be explicitly defined in each case by the Council.

9.   A permanent Commission shall be constituted to receive and examine the annual reports of the Mandatories and to advise the Council on all matters relating to the observance of the mandates.

Article 23

Subject to and in accordance with the provisions of international conventions existing or hereafter to be agreed upon, the Members of the League:

(a)   will endeavour to secure and maintain fair and humane conditions of labour for men, women, and children, both in their own countries and in all countries to which their commercial and industrial relations extend, and for that purpose will establish and maintain the necessary international organizations:

(b)   undertake to secure just treatment of the native inhabitants of territories under their control;

(c)   will entrust the League with the general supervision over the execution of agreements with regard to the traffic in women and children, and the traffic in opium and other dangerous drugs;

(d) will entrust the League with the general supervision of the trade in arms and ammunition with the countries in which the control of this traffic is necessary in the common interest;

(e) will make provision to secure and maintain freedom of communications and of transit and equitable treatment for the commerce of all Members of the League. In this connexion, the special necessities of the regions devastated during the war of 1914-1918 shall be borne in mind;

(f) will endeavour to take steps in matters of international concern for the prevention and control of disease.

Article 24

1.   There shall be placed under the direction of the League all international bureaux already established by general treaties if the parties to such treaties consent. All such international bureaux and all commissions for the regulation of matters of international interest hereafter constituted shall be placed under the direction of the League.

2.   In all matters of international interest which are regulated by general conventions but which are not placed under the control of international bureaux or commissions, the Secretariat of the League shall, subject to the consent of the Council and if desired by the parties, collect and distribute all relevant information and shall render any other assistance which may be necessary or desirable.

3.   The Council may include as part of the expenses of the Secretariat the expenses of any bureaux or commission which is placed under the direction of the League.

Article 25

The Members of the League agree to encourage and promote the establishment and co-operation of duly authorized voluntary national Red Cross organizations having as purposes the improvement of health, the prevention of disease and the mitigation of suffering throughout the world.

Article 26

1.   Amendments to this Covenant will take effect when ratified by the Members of the League whose Representatives compose the Council and by a majority of the Members of the League whose Representatives compose the Assembly.

2.   No such amendment shall bind any Member of the League which signifies its dissent therefrom, but in that case it shall cease to be a Member of the League.

Membership of League

THE 61 STATES WHO JOINED THE LEAGUE
(Between 1919 and 1939)

Abyssinia	Ecuador	Mexico
Afghanistan	Egypt	Netherlands
Albania	Estonia	New Zealand
Argentina	Finland	Norway
Australia	France	Panama
Austria	Germany*	Paraguay*
Belgium	Greece	Peru
Bolivia	Guatemala	Poland
Brazil*	Haiti	Portugal
Britain	Honduras	Russia*
Bulgaria	Hungary	Salvador*
Canada	India	Siam
Chile*	Iran	Spain*
China	Iraq	South Africa
Colombia	Ireland	Sweden
Costa Rica	Japan*	Switzerland
Cuba	Latvia	Italy*
Czechoslovakia	Liberia	Turkey
Denmark	Lithuania	Uruguay
Dominica	Luxembourg	Venezuela*
		Yugoslavia

* These ten members left, or gave notice of leaving, on various dates.

Further Reading List

Aberg, S. E.: *Woodrow Wilson and the League of Nations* (Scholastic) 1966.

Bendiner, E.: *A Time for Angels* (Knopf) 1975.

Birdsall, P.: *Versailles, Twenty Years After* (Allen & Unwin) 1941.

Carr, E. H.: *The Twenty Years Crisis* (Macmillan) 1939.

Dexter, B.: *The Years of Opportunity* (Viking) 1967.

Devlin, D.: *Too Proud to Fight* (Oxford) 1975.

Eichelberger, C. M.: *Organising for Peace* (Harper & Row) 1977.

Foley, H.: *Woodrow Wilson's Case for the League* (Princeton) 1923.

Fosdick, Raymond: *The League of Nations and the United Nations* (New York) 1971.

Grey, Lord: *Twenty-Five Years* (World) 1926.

Jenks, Wilfred: *The World Beyond the Charter* (Allen & Unwin) 1969.

Joyce, J. Avery: *End of an Illusion* (Allen & Unwin) 1969.

Joyce, J. Avery: *Story of International Co-operation* (Watts, New York) 1967.

Joyce, J. Avery:	*World Organization* (Watts, London) 1944.
Keynes, J. M.:	*Economic Consequences of Peace* (Oxford) 1922.
Lederer, I. J.:	*The Versailles Settlement* (Heath) 1966.
Link, A. S.:	*Woodrow Wilson, A Profile* (Hill & Wang) 1968.
Loveday, A.:	*Reflections on International Administration* (Oxford) 1950.
Madariaga, S. de:	*The World's Design* (Allen & Unwin) 1938.
Miller, D. H.:	*Drafting of the Covenant* (Putman) 1928.
Myers, D. P.:	*Handbook of the League of Nations* (Boston) 1935.
Noel-Baker, P. J.:	*League of Nations at Work* (Nisbet, London) 1927.
Nicolson, H.:	*Peacemaking, 1919* (Grosset & Dunlop) 1965.
Ranshofen-Wertheimer, E. F.:	*The International Secretariat* (Carnegie) 1945.
Rappard, W. E.:	*The Geneva Experiment* (Oxford) 1931.
Reynolds, E. E.:	*The League Experiment* (Nelson) 1938.
Seaman, L. C. B.:	*From Vienna to Versailles* (Harper & Row) 1955.
Scott, G.:	*The Rise and Fall of the League of Nations* (Hutchinson) 1973.
Swanwick, H. M.:	*Collective Insecurity* (Cape, London) 1937.
Taylor, A. J. P.:	*From Sarajevo to Potsdam* (Harcourt, Brace) 1966.
Toynbee, A. J.:	*The World After the Peace Conference* (Oxford) 1926.

Traz, R. de: *The Spirit of Geneva* (Oxford) 1935.

Tuchman, B.: *Guns of August* (Dell) 1963.

Vallentin, A.: *Stresemann's Race with Death* (Constable) 1931.

"Vigilantes": *Inquest on Peace* (Gollancz) 1935.

Walters, F. P.: *A History of the League of Nations* (Oxford) 1952.

Watt, R. M.: *The Kings Depart* (Simon & Schuster) 1968.

Williams, J. F.: *Some Aspects of the Covenant* (Oxford) 1934.

Zimmern, A.: *The League of Nations and the Rule of Law* (Macmillan) 1936.

Index